LINCOLN CHRISTIAN COLL

P9-CDF-439

Come Sunday

THE LITURGY OF Zion

A Companion to Songs of Zion

Come Sunday

THE LITURGY OF Zion

William B. McClain

Abingdon Press
Nashville

COME SUNDAY: THE LITURGY OF ZION

Copyright © 1990 by Abingdon Press.

All rights reserved.
No part of this work may be reproduced or transmitted in any form
or by any means, electronic or mechanical, including photocopying
and recording, or by any information storage or retrieval system,
except as may be expressly permitted by the 1976 Copyright Act or
in writing from the publisher. Requests for permission should be
addressed in writing to Abingdon Press, 201 Eighth Avenue South,
Nashville, TN 37203.

This book is printed on recycled, acid-free paper.

Come Sunday: The Liturgy of Zion

Library of Congress Cataloging-in-Publication Data

MCCLAIN, WILLIAM B.
   Come Sunday: the liturgy of Zion / by William B. McClain.
      p.   cm.
   Includes bibliographical references.
   ISBN 0-687-08884-4 (alk. paper)
   1. Afro-Americans—Religion. 2. Sunday. 3. Liturgics—United States. 4.
Afro-American preaching. 5. Black theology. 6. Songs of Zion. 7. Hymns,
English—United States—History and criticism. 8. Afro-Americans—
Music. 9. United Methodist Church (U.S.)—Hymns. 10. Methodist
Church—United States—Hymns. I. Title.
BR563.N4M33   1990
264'.076'008996073—dc20   90-33549
                                                                  CIP

97 98 99 00 01 02 03 04—10 9 8 7 6 5 4

MANUFACTURED IN THE UNITED STATES OF AMERICA

To the memory of
Judge Jefferson Cleveland
who helped the church
and the world sing the *Songs of Zion*.

and

To Cousin Cathaleen Coates
who taught me the songs

and

My sisters Helen, Catherine, Dorothy, and Juliet
who first sang them with me.

111386

Come Sunday, oh, come Sunday
that's the day.
Lord, dear Lord above,
God almighty, God of love,
Please look down and see my people through.

—*Duke Ellington*

Come Sunday, by Duke Ellington
Copyright © 1946 (Renewed) G. Schirmer, Inc.
International Copyright Secured. All rights reserved.

Contents

Foreword

We are a singing people! We have a song when we may have little else. We seem to sing at the strangest times when song to the outside observer seems inappropriate, such as when we are sad.

In our melancholy, our songs are not always mournful songs. Most often, they are joyous, lifting the spirit above despair.

Yet, our sad songs sometimes come in the midst of our joy, in moments of jubilation and celebration. Without warning caution emerges to remind us that songs of joy must be tempered by the stark realities of the plight of our people. In the midst of our joyful singing the soul has not forgotten depression, pain, and expressions of hopelessness on the faces of our young. Laughter turns to tears and our glad songs into laments.

But we refuse to give up or give in. There is this God-sense that has become a part of the fabric of the race. We refuse to let God alone, and we know God has never let us alone! At the moment of our deepest despair we sing, "sometimes I feel like a motherless child a long way from home." Then, in the midst of our sadness, we sing with assurance, "I'm so glad that trouble don't last always!"

Song is so much a part of the black community. Music is

the carrier of our history and faith as much as the spoken or written word. Music gives hope and sustains us. Ours is a diverse music—both African and American, simple and profound, traditional and contemporary. Its theology is so far ranging as to defy categorization. It is at once conservative and liberal, of this world but not constrained by it.

As much as we are a singing people, we are a demonstrative people. We are in touch with ourselves, our bodies. We are full of our senses, utilizing them all. We do not merely walk for instance; we strut, we glide. Actors of the highest order are we, seeing life as high drama, and we play the many roles as in Greek drama. We move in and out of these with dexterity that confounds the so-called wise. From maid to matron, butler to baron, from anonymity to celebrity, from "nobody" to "somebody."

Only the casual observer fails to see the rich drama in our ritual and liturgy. Worship in the black church is both ordered and free, formal and informal. There is "plenty good room" for order and spontaneity.

We revel in pomp and circumstance. Color and pageantry characterize our worship more than simplicity and blandness. We march, dance, wave, shout, nod, genuflect. We of all people make a joyful noise unto the Lord. Liturgy for us is not what we do; it is what we are. We cannot separate it from ourselves and hence from our worship. We are liturgical people. Most of all we are authentic.

If there is any word that most accurately describes the worship of the black church, it is authenticity. We stumble only when we try to be other than ourselves.

What this book does is to remind those who have forgotten this rich liturgical history and to inform those who never knew, of the power and potential of worship in the black religious experience. It shows us from where we've come, and points us to where we must go if the church of the future is to be as relevant as the church of the past.

It carries the user through the seasons of the Christian year, as well as through the struggles and joys of a people. It combines our African past with the black American experience, enriched by the experience of other racial and ethnic traditions.

This is not a book only for black people. Rather, it offers insights for all who sing the songs of Zion in their own way. It is fundamentally a book about hope and faith for all God's children, who dwell in a weary land and summons all— white, black, Asian, Hispanic, Native American, Euro- pean, African, Latin American to "walk together children" as you sing the songs of Zion.

Woodie W. White, Bishop
Illinois Area
The United Methodist Church

Acknowledgments

This book was made possible by a grant from the General Board of Discipleship of The United Methodist Church because of its continued interest in strengthening the worship life of the church. It was that same board along with other individuals and agencies with whom I worked to produce the *Songs of Zion* songbook in 1981. Its interest in the ethnic contribution to enrich worship continues to be substantial. I received substantial financial and administrative support from the Ethnic Minority Local Church office and the Section on Worship of the General Board of Discipleship. Dr. David White, Assistant General Secretary of that board for Ethnic Minority Local Church, has worked hard and long to see that *The Liturgy of Zion* issue forth in an authentic, practical, solid publication for use to strengthen the local church. And his efforts have been supported by the Rev. Andy Langford and Dr. Hoyt L. Hickman of the Section on Worship. Their counsel, support and untiring efforts are acknowledged here with deep gratitude.

The United Methodist Publishing House and Abingdon Press contributed editorial and publishing help. Particular thanks go to Dr. Robert Feaster, publisher; Mr. Neil Alexander, general manager/editorial director; and especially to Dr. Ronald P. Patterson, senior editor, whose creative help and support enabled this book to reach publication.

For their tremendous contribution to this effort and for their sound advice and unstinting support throughout the life of this project, I gratefully acknowledge a National Advisory Committee representing all sections of the church: Dr. Zan Holmes, Dallas, Texas; Ms. Betty Henderson, Philadelphia, Pennsylvania; Dr. Douglass E. Fitch, Los Angeles, California; the Rev. Tallulah Fisher-Williams, Chicago, Illinois; Dr. William Farley Smith, New York, New York; Dr. John Corry, Nashville, Tennessee; and Dr. Edward E. Bufford, Jamaica, New York.

My gratitude goes to several secretaries who cheerfully helped me in all stages of this book: Mrs. Martha E. Stewart, Mrs. Rachel Blue, Ms. Deborah Thomas, and Ms. Corietta Israel. My debt to all of them is greater than I can say in these pages. Special thanks, also, to Jacqui Burton of the Lilly Foundation for financial assistance.

My deep gratitude goes to a number of consultants who offered their expertise and research skills: Dr. C. Eric Lincoln, Dr. John C. Diamond, Mrs. Jessie Mae Robinson (who provided her files of considerable volumes on liturgies of Zion), Mrs. Cynthia Felder (who did extensive research on the gospel songs and other materials), the Rev. Bruce Haskins, Mrs. Juliet M. Hart, the Rev. Carmen R. Collette, Mrs. Elsie Thomas, and Mr. Justus Reeves.

I owe a tremendous debt of thanks to Dr. Laurence H. Stookey, my colleague and friend at Wesley Theological Seminary. He was constantly available for consultation, advice, suggestions and comfort. He is largely responsible for preparing the indexes and wrote much of Chapter VIII, *"Songs of Zion* and Liturgical Time." His contribution to this work is substantial.

A special word of thanks is offered to Mrs. J. LaVon Wilson, who was always willing to make her rich resources available and to offer valuable suggestions. Particular thanks goes to Mr. Gloster Current; and to Mrs. Charlotte

Meade, who seemed to have always thought about the *Liturgy of Zion* before I could ask about it. A very special word of thanks is offered to Bishop Woodie White, schoolmate and long-time respected friend, who graciously agreed to write the foreword to this book.

In this work, as in all other, my wife, Jo Ann Mattos McClain, has been supportive. She read every word of this book and offered valuable suggestions. Words of gratitude are not adequate to express my deep appreciation.

It is my hope that the *communal* nature of this project has made for a better book. That is certainly in keeping with the spirit of the people whose legacy we inherit and who made and make possible such a rich tradition.

This is not a book simply for Black Methodists. Nor is it a book written just for black people. Rather, it is written for people who are interested in the black worship tradition and who seek new, and perhaps different ways, to praise God and to enter into God's courts with thanksgiving. It is about the diversity of black worship: simple and profound, conservative and liberal, formal and informal, traditional and contemporary. But in its deepest and most authentic sense, a soulful acknowledgment of the faith taught by the past, hopeful and grateful for the gift of life in the present, and encouraging about facing the future to be a part of what *God* and *we* can do when we walk together. Therefore, it is a book for all who are pilgrims in a weary land, and for those who can even imagine a God who draws straight with crooked lines. It is a book for the worship leader and the worshipper—liturgical or non-liturgical. It was written to be used to explore a people's religious response to oppression, and the creative, soulful ways they sought worth, meaning, dignity and hope in the face of an idolatrous chauvinism with the bruising chancre of racism lacerating their very souls.

This book is offered as a worship resource, textbook, study book, history book and resource in black religion. It is hoped that it will be used by local churches, worship committees, scholars, district and regional groups, college and seminary classes, in worship, history, and cultural studies, youth fellowships, and by many others. It is written as an aid to *Songs of Zion* (Nashville: Abingdon Press, 1981), but can also be read and studied on its own. The advice of the advisory committee was crystal clear: *"a scholarly, practical, authentically black book."*

William B. McClain
Oxon Hill, Maryland
April 30, 1990

I

Introduction: God Sends Sunday

God Sends Sunday is the title of a novel by Arna Bontemps, written in 1931. Although I have not read the book for many years and scarcely remember the details, I am still sure about the profound meaning of the title. In the black church and the black community everything leads to and is planned around Sunday. Not only is it the first day of the week or the Sabbath Day, it is the chief day of the week. It is the day of the week for which all other days prepare, and it is the day that prepares the people to make it through all the other days. Sunday gives the stability to the week and provides the fulcrum for organizing the week, the month and the year. For the faithful it is a day they may depend on for "pure water and strong wine" when they are "athirst in the Sahara of . . . meaninglessness."

It is a major thesis of this book that Sunday is the central day in the black church and the black community. I emphasize the black church *and* the black community because there is no discontinuity on importance of Sunday. It is true of both the sacred and the secular. Chapter II, "Come Sunday," attempts to show the reasons why Sunday remains the premier day in black North America. Beginning with slavery and tracing it through the present, we shall explore the importance of Sunday. There are clear

21

historical and social reasons, but there is also theological and biblical ground for the special significance of "the Lord's Day" in the black community. Perhaps this practice can become a challenge to rescue the Christian faith from the liturgical inertia and Sunday "ho-hum" prevalent in many quarters of the church—even, if it is experienced vicariously.

To understand the religious history of a people is to know their social habits, their politics, their hopes and aspirations, their fears, their failures, their understanding of who they are and what they value most. While there is a distinct history of black people and their religion in North America, that development cannot be properly understood without an awareness of the externals and the world around them, which shaped their sense of reality. The chancre of racism in this country has been a catalyst in stunting Christianity in North America. This idolatrous chauvinism must be seen as part of the external which shaped the founding and the forming of the black church. If there had been no racism, there probably would not have been a black church.

Chapter III, "The Black Church: A Mirror of Tragedy and a Vision of Hope," traces the history of the black church and offers some background to help explain the spiritual response of black people to this American dilemma. When the Christian faith flowed through the souls of black folk, a new worship style developed—the liturgy of Zion, which is neither African nor European, but a black American style. That style gives rise to the songs of the soil and of the soul and to a prophetic stance in preaching. These form the corpus of the *Liturgy of Zion*.

Chapters IV and V explore the body of material that constitutes the *Liturgy of Zion*. Chapter IV, subtitled "The Soul of Black Worship," looks at the uniqueness of worship in the black tradition and reshaping the worship the slaves heard through the windows of white churches when their numbers grew too large to seat them in the galleries or balconies.

Black worship is not merely a replica of white worship nor the reenactment of African tribal rituals, but a third entity created to offer refulgence to a people weary at heart. Its liturgy and theology are derived from the cultural and religious experience of a people struggling to appropriate the meaning of God and human life in the midst of suffering. This tradition encouraged celebrating the power to survive and affirming life with all of its contradictory realities. Spontaneity and improvisations are necessary corollaries in such a tradition.

This chapter also examines ritual and song. Seeing worship as drama, the author explores the importance of fellowship and community in Afro-American religious life. And, there *is* ritual: with long choir processionals, specified procedures for ushers, and starched and ironed white uniforms for the communion stewards. Many black churches even have marches to bring the tithes and offerings to the altar. These dramatic rites are repeated week after week with a good deal of precision and care.

The black church is a *singing* church. No worship is planned or executed without music. It is as close to worship as breathing is to life. Anyone who understands an African background of chanting, drumming, dancing and intoning will not marvel that even medium-sized churches may have five or six choirs or choral groups performing different kinds of music in a worship service. As Hortense Spillers has rightly observed:

> Singing, scarcely less than preaching is a central aspect of black worship, joining the preacher and his congregation in a spiritual unity which momentarily transcends the hardships and injustices of this world, humanizing the social order indeed, and making it bearable.[1]

This fact accounts for the need for *Songs of Zion* and the reason it is used by churches of all sizes, locations, styles and denominations.

Chapter V is devoted to black preaching and is sub-titled "Is There Any Word From the Lord?" taken from Jeremiah 37:17. The black church expects the sermon to answer that question every Sunday, every season. Even when the preacher cannot say it with eloquence or conviction, and even when the preacher does not seem to know what it is, or *how* to proclaim it, the congregation knows there *is* a Word from the Lord. They seek and expect it. It's Sunday, the day of His rising and our rising, a weekly celebration of the Savior's victory, the hope on which the faith is built; and they seek to hear that Word from the pulpit.

They know it is the same Word: "God was in Christ reconciling the world. . . ." making whole again all that is shattered, filling all who are empty, giving strength to the weak, courage to the fainthearted and calling all who are wicked and away to come home to God's family. They know that. They know that in Christ we find one who loves the unlovable, who takes the inevitability out of history, and who meets justice at Calvary's brow. They know that Calvary's hill is higher than Capitol Hill. They know that Christ makes the crooked straight and smooths the rough places; and they come to hear it again and again, because they hunger for the lively Word *fitly* spoken—with an accent on fitly spoken.

Chapter V explains what is meant by "fitly spoken" in black preaching. It echoes the congregation's plea for the Word to be preached with power and passion and preparation, to set at liberty both the *captors* and the *captives*. God sends Sunday. No *Liturgy of Zion* is complete, and we have not *had* church until the Word has been preached and the people are able to join in one voice, and say "A-men!"

Chapter VI moves into the second part of this book and relates specifically to *Songs of Zion*. Some may see this section as the more practical aspect of the book. But nothing presented here is in conflict with what has gone before.

Chapter VI begins with a survey of the various songs contained in *Songs of Zion*: Negro spirituals, hymns, gospel songs. For each type of song we offer suggestions about their use and performance. Much of this section was prepared in consultation with Dr. J. Jefferson Cleveland, the principal editor of *Songs of Zion*, before his untimely death. The suggestions here are greatly enhanced by his wide knowledge, considerable experience as a performer, composer, teacher and minister of church music, and by his never-ending love for the church and its church music.

Chapter VII deals with the *"Songs of Zion* and Liturgical Time'' as a way of strengthening the *Liturgy of Zion* during Lenten-Easter and Advent-Christmas. Each Sunday is reviewed with the appropriate themes and specific hymns from *Songs of Zion* are suggested. If followed, these suggestions can help us to celebrate Sunday more fully and to *relive* the seasons of the gospel.

Chapter VIII is devoted exclusively to the Negro spirituals because of their importance to the black church and black history and because of their wide-ranging contribution to possibilities in worship. Many interpreters of the spirituals have been consulted. Obviously there is *no one* way of interpreting the Negro spirituals. I hope these comments will encourage their use and further study of deep and abiding meaning.

The emphasis here has been primarily on the gospel song composer-arranger, since biographies of hymn writers can be easily found in hymn book companions. In each case the entries included in *Songs of Zion* are cited. In some cases, performance suggestions and additional information about the composition are included.

There are two indexes in this book: a topical index and a scriptural reference index. These will be especially helpful with the lectionary, but not exclusively. They provide a way of finding and giving continuity to the services of worship whether the lectionary is used or not. They can help the planner of worship to focus on the Lord's acts of grace and proclaim the gospel of salvation. A discography is provided for specific examples of creative interpretation of gospel songs by both pioneers and contemporary artists. These may be listened to to *catch* the gospel sound.

The ideas in this book have been shared in lectures, workshops, local churches, schools, and consultations across the country. Chapters IV and V in different forms were delivered as lectures at Duke University, The Divinity School, Durham, North Carolina; St. Paul School of Theology, Kansas City, Missouri; and Wesley Theological Seminary, Washington, D.C. Various gatherings of Black Methodists for Church Renewal across the church have offered their suggestions and criticisms. The United Methodist Hymnal Revision Committee listened to parts of Chapter VI and offered their comments. These pastors, lay people, students and colleagues have heard me. I hope I have heard them and their valuable comments.

One other word: the only intent for writing this book is to try to offer some help in appreciating the *Liturgy of Zion* in relationship to the *Songs of Zion*.

Come Sunday, oh, come Sunday
that's the day,
Lord, dear Lord above,
God almighty, God of love,
Please look down and see my people through.
                                    —*Duke Ellington*

Come Sunday

The Importance of Sunday

It's Sunday morning in Savannah and it's time for church. Sunday in Savannah is just like Sunday in Atlanta or New York or New Orleans or Yamacraw or Yazoo City.

There is no more important day in the North American black community than Sunday. That is true of *every* Sunday—*any* Sunday—*anywhere* in black America. Perhaps that is true of all Christians, but it's especially true of black people, whether they are Christian or not. It is convincingly so, if they are. Some very concrete social, historical and cultural reasons may exist for *why* Sunday is the time to have church; but, the reasons are also theological, biblical and liturgical. It may be just because Sunday is "The Lord's Day," and "ordinariness" or any "ordinary time" just doesn't happen on Sunday. If there is an error of liturgy, it's that there are not enough Sundays that allow for quiet reflection. But it's Sunday and that has an importance all its own.

──────

*Come Sunday, by Duke Ellington, Copyright © 1946 (Renewed) G. Schirmer, Inc. International Copyright secured. All rights reserved.

The importance of Sunday is seen in almost every aspect of black life. Secular music reflects the importance of Sunday. One can hear a deeply serious Nina Simone crooning "One More Sunday Morning in Savannah," and hear her add to the song, "in Savannah, in Atlanta, it's the same thing"; or Lou Rawls singing, "The eagle flies on Friday, and Saturday I go out to play. But Sunday, I go to church and pray: 'Lord, have mercy,' ''; or a hundred blues singers intoning: "I want a *Sunday* kind of love." Sunday is a special day, every week, every month, every year.

Sunday provides a way of keeping time. The black church and the black community refer to the "first Sunday" or the "fourth Sunday" instead of the date or the season. How many times does one hear, "Our Homecoming is the third Sunday in August," or "our Youth Day is the fifth Sunday in June." No reference to the date is given. The date *is* the third Sunday or the fifth Sunday and everybody will know when that is.

Sunday and Slavery: Time on the Cross

Sunday became an important day for the slaves even though they were doing time on a cross—forced to work from sunup to sundown planting, plowing, picking and pleasing. One needed a *sun* day to gather with others and to rest, rejoice, release, and be refreshed, and to celebrate being simply human. After all, even masters and owners tried to be more human to the slaves on Sunday. A former slave recalled her experience in *Lay My Burden Down:*

> We went to church every Sunday. We had both white and colored preachers. Master Frank wasn't a Christian, but he would help build brush arbors for us to have church under and we sure would have big meetings, I'll tell you.[1]

For some slaves, it was not merely a matter of Christmas when you got special privileges, gifts, special foods, and favors. That was good; however Christmas came only once a year. Sunday came every week; and that day was special —a regular time to anticipate. Nicey Kinney, an ex-slave in Jackson County, Georgia, remembered the scene and described it:

> They would go in big crowds, and sometimes a far piece off. They was all fixed up in their Sunday clothes, and they walked barefoot with their shoes about their shoulders, to keep 'em from getting dirty. Just 'fore they got to the church they stopped and put on their shoes, and they was ready to git together to hear the preacher.[2]

Not only was Sunday a time to put down the hammer and hoe and lift up the Christ of the cross, but it was also a day to get rid of work clothes, rules, bosses and to don your best clothes and manners and go and *have* church. Until this very day, many black people still use the expression "to *have* church." A former slave in Alabama recalled the festival nature of Sunday and the importance of the day:

> My God, child, people never know nothing but to go to church on Sunday. I think that was the finest thing. I know for me and my grandfather to walk fourteen miles to church over there on the hill every Sunday. I remember we would set out 'bout time the sun would be rising . . . we would carry our dinner with us 'cause we know we would be till night getting back home again. . . .[3]

For the slaves, it was a chance to go where there was recognition and respect; here everybody was somebody. It was an opportunity to hear hope reaffirmed, to sing about a Jesus who understood their world of trials, tribulations, suffering, and oppression, and to be reassured of a time and an age "when every day will be Sunday." It was also a time to know that the God of Moses, Abraham, Joshua, and

Jesus was the same God of the oppressed who cares about and would deliver these weary travellers. And God would, in time, deliver them to a better place—if not here and now, then surely "by and by."

It was a time and a place to sing and pray and preach and shout. These gatherings of a subjugated people on Sundays most likely lasted longer than one hour. Perhaps these weekly events masked a sublimated outrage balanced with patience, cheerfulness and a boundless trust in the ultimate victory of God's justice over sin, death and oppression— even though they were doing their time on the cross.

It was Sunday now, and "A Great Camp Meeting" (#156) existed where they could sing, pray, preach and shout and never tire. It was a day and a time and a place to lay burdens down.

The Importance of Time in Christian Worship

What began with the slaves as a practical and human need for Sunday is not obvious theologically. Time is crucial in the Christian faith and worship. Our understanding of God is tied to events that occur within history, particularly the events of Jesus' birth, baptism, ministry, suffering, and death. His resurrection, ascension, and reign in glory are indications of his entrance into a new kind of existence that transforms the present; even so, this new existence is thought of in terms of time. It is a new age, which we now anticipate and in which we shall one day participate.

Thus as we join worship in the present, with one hand we grasp the past and with the other hand we take hold of the future, so that time is bound together in God's wholeness. No wonder Christians, like Jews before them, set aside particular times for worship, weekly assemblies of the congregation as well as annual observances. But Sunday is the primary festival day of the church, not simply Christmas or Easter or any other special day that comes but once a year.

The Nineteenth Century hymn, "O Day of Rest and Gladness" states the case concisely and very well:

> On thee, at the creation
>   the light first had its birth;
> On thee, for our salvation
>   Christ rose from depths of earth;
> On the, the Lord victorious
>   the Spirit send from heaven;
> And thus on thee most glorious
>   a triple light was given.[4]

("Thee" refers not to God, but to Sunday.)

Commenting on the point of the hymn and the importance of Sunday as the chief festival day of the church, Dr. Laurence H. Stookey observes:

> Sunday is the premier day of worship because it is a perpetual commemoration of (1) the light God called forth on the first day of creation; (2) the triumph of the Light of the World over sin and death through his resurrection on the first day of the week; (3) the enlightenment of the Apostles when the Holy Spirit formed church on the Day of Pentecost. Whenever we gather as People of God, what the hymn writer refers to as this 'triple light' calls forth from us (implicitly, if not explicitly) the prayer 'Let the Heav'n Light Shine on Me' (#218).[5]

The Black Church and "The Lord's Day"

In the last twenty-five years there has been great emphasis on the lectionary, liturgical reform, and the observance of the Christian year. Some have thought the idea of reliving the seasons of the gospel as new and different, while others have resisted it as a creation of those

31

who want to be more like Roman Catholics. However, celebrating the Christian year is neither new nor exclusively Roman Catholic. It is simply the church's way of keeping time.

The early church kept time by believing in the signs of Jesus' birth, baptism, ministry, suffering, death, Resurrection, and ascension. It was the faith of the church that the Resurrection was the central act of God. Each of the Gospels reveals that the empty tomb was discovered on the morning of the first day: the day creation had begun and the moment God had "separated light from darkness." Their point was to make certain the importance of the Lord's Day by linking it to creation and the Resurrection.

By the second century, "the Lord's Day" had become a Christian term for good reasons: Paul urged the Corinthian Christians to "lay aside" money for the collection on the first day of the week (I Corinthians 16:2). John, the Revelator, lets us know that he was "in the Spirit on the Lord's day" (Revelation 1:10). Paul was at Troas talking until midnight Saturday, but broke bread with the Christians when Sunday came (Acts 20:7 and 11).

But the pagan term "Sunday" (which means the rising of the sun) became linked to the Lord's Day by comparing Christ's rising from the dead to the rising of the sun. In about 155 A.D., Justin Martyr baptized the term into the Christian faith in his words to a pagan audience: "We all hold this common gathering on Sunday since it is the first day, on which God, transforming darkness and matter, made the universe, and Jesus Christ our Savior rose from the dead on the same day."[6] In the Epistle of St. Barnabas, Sunday is called "an eighth day, that is the beginning of another world . . . in which Jesus also rose from the dead.'"[7] These themes of a new creation and light become significant images in the Christian celebration of Sunday as the day of resurrection. Sunday is the weekly anniversary of the Lord's rising. It is the Lord's Day: a day of new creation, new beginning, the day of the sun risen from darkness.

The black church is on solid biblical and theological ground in not losing the importance of the Lord's Day. Part of what scholars of liturgical theology and the New Testament are saying to our contemporary world is: "Let's recover the significance of the Lord's Day."[8] *The black church never lost it.* There is no day, season, festival, or observance more important than Sunday, the chief day of rest and worship, a day of celebration. This fact continues to be a constant strength in the black tradition. While practical reasons, or an accident of history, or the circumstances of slavery and suffering may have made the black church and community place this overwhelming significance on Sunday as the "day of rest and gladness," they were soundly at one with the practice of the early church and the admonitions and spirit of the New Testament. Maybe it is the way of an oppressed people, a suffering minority.

But then, one is driven back to see that those first Christians, also an oppressed minority. Not only did they know about the Lord's Calvary, they were persecuted and crucified daily. They lived constantly with the possibility of being just another sporting meal for the lions. But they walked to martyrdom with faith in a resurrected Lord who had conquered the powers of death and had left an empty tomb on Sunday. And even though they sometimes had to meet before daybreak on the Lord's Day, ("an appointed day" as Pliny, the Roman administrator, noticed), "it was their custom to meet and to break bread together." Pliny probably did not understand why they met, but had he asked them, they would have told him: because it was the Lord's Day. It was Sunday, the day of resurrection. It was a day to remember the Lord and the mighty acts of God, and especially to commemorate the Lord's suffering, death, and resurrection. But most important of all, it was the day on which the Savior rose from the dead. Each Sunday is the anniversary of the Resurrection.

33

And perhaps the slaves would have offered a similar answer: "He 'rose from the dead and the Lord will bear my spirit home!" (#168) and therefore I've got to "steal away to Jesus" (#134) because "my Lord calls me."

But what was true then is still true of the black church as it gathers from Sunday to Sunday. It is the Lord's day and a time to "Lift Him Up" (#59).

He'll lift you up
if you ask Him,
He'll show you the way.
He'll fill your cup,
if you ask Him,
He'll brighten your day,
if you ask Him. (#186)

For "We are our heavenly Father's children and we all know that He loves us one and all . . . for he knows just how much we can bear." (#202)

The Liturgy of Zion and the Lectionary

The use of the lectionary is a way of reading our way through various sections of scripture, week by week in an organized manner. It is a way of reliving the seasons of the gospel of our Lord, organizing our worship life and focusing our praise and thanksgiving. The lectionary helps maintain a balanced variety of preaching and worship themes related to God's present action in our world. But its use is not antithetical to what we have said earlier about the importance of Sunday itself or the chief festival day. Nor must the use of aids in planning worship undercut the essential importance of every Sunday in the black worship tradition.

Some comments and suggestions can be made about the use of the lectionary and the various liturgical seasons, but nothing should obscure the fact that God is at work in unusual and ordinary ways. Every Sunday is a Sunday to identify divine grace in every circumstance of life. Part of being a Christian is seeing God at work where others may perceive "ordinariness" or even what seems to be God's absence. Every Sunday is a time for affirming that:

There's not an hour that He is not near us.
No night so dark but His love can cheer us.
(#38, stanza 3)

Black Christians have been especially aware that to be Christian is to be "Easter People" (#6). How many times when the way gets dark and dreary, the road rough and rocky, the problems great and discouraging, the black preacher has reminded a beleaguered and discouraged flock: "It's Friday now, but Sunday's coming"! Christians do not remain at the cross where crucifixion and death hold sway. Part of the great contribution of the black worship and preaching tradition has been not only to face realistically the burdens and troubles of this world, but to find the grace notes in a sad song, to affirm hope in the midst of debilitating despair, to find a "bright side somewhere." That bright side for black Christians, and all who will believe, is on the other side of the empty tomb, beyond Friday—because Sunday does come!

III

The Black Church: A Mirror of Tragedy and a Vision of Hope

In the black church going to church is more than attending a worship service. It is a way of gathering all of what the people are; the event brings the spiritual response of the community to the experience of suffering. Going to church offers a way of deciphering the meaning of living life in relation to God and neighbor. It is a time to reflect and to provide ways the human spirit can transcend the multifarious conditions of racial oppression. The occasion allows the African gods to die and give way to the God of Christianity, while maintaining some sense of identity and junction between the present and the past. The experience permits a time of finding meaning, worth, hope, and purpose in new and different contexts. It is a time for celebrating survival and freedom and renewing hope. No part of the task of living is barred, for in the black community the church has been that one institution which touches all of life. It is uniquely claimed as belonging to the people—even to non-members and strangers.

It is against the backdrop of American racism, a peculiarly heinous and an idolatrous chauvinism, that the transplanted Africans began in slavery to develop a spiritual response to their suffering human condition. Since at first there was not any serious or overriding concern to convert to Christianity these black wards recently fetched from Africa, they were left to their own resources. The majority of black North Americans practiced whatever fragments of African religions they could remember, modified, of course, by the particular mixture of tribes and the particular exigencies of life on the given plantation. Seen as heathen ritual and dismissed as childish superstitions, these expressions of African religions were forbidden, and whenever possible, slaves who came from the same tribe or spoke the same language were separated from each other and sold off to distant plantations.

Christianizing the Africans

For almost a century black North Americans had little or no contact with American Christianity. From the landing of the first Africans at Jamestown in 1619 until the Society for the Propagation of the Faith began its work of evangelizing the slaves in 1701, black salvation remained outside the concerns of North American Christians. By contrast, in Brazil, Jamaica, Haiti, the Caribbean, and South America less rigid social structures allowed contact with tribal groups and the mixture of Christianity and varied forms of African religions. Among the Caribbean, South American, and the Maroon slave populations, distinctive cultural traits survived for centuries almost untouched. But when Christianity was introduced to the slaves of North America, due in part to high and relentless contact with their masters and in part to a desire to make Christianity the servant of the masters' agenda, slaves enthusiastically embraced Christianity, in particular the Protestant traditions, and suppressed their ancient religious practices.

With the coming of the Great Awakening, with its outdoor camp meetings and revivals, around 1740 the black masses along with the poor white farmers, the working class, and the declassed masses, responded passionately

38

and enthusiastically to a simple gospel of grace. These were sincere and profound religious experiences, as the black slaves heard of a God who knew the sufferings of his children. Poverty was no barrier to membership; the poorest were made most welcome.

Great numbers flocked to hear this good news and expressed their feelings with cries, shouts, tears, prostrations, convulsions, and other physical and emotional responses. The God of *feelings* took on real significance for the slaves and provided a perspective on the faith that bore promise of true spiritual utility.

Richard Allen, the founder of the African Methodist Episcopal Church, tells of his conversion in 1777, typical of such dramatic conversions:

> I was (he said) awakened and brought to see myself, poor, wretched and undone, and without the mercy of God must be lost. Shortly after, I obtained mercy through the blood of Christ, and was constrained to exhort my old companies to seek the Lord. I went rejoicing for several days and was happy in the Lord, in conversing with many old, experienced Christians. I was brought under doubts, and was tempted to believe I was deceived, and was constrained to seek the Lord afresh. I went with my head bowed down for many days. My sins were a heavy burden. I was tempted to believe there was no mercy for me. I cried to the Lord both night and day. One night I thought hell would be my portion. I cried unto Him who delighteth to hear the prayers of a poor sinner, and all of a sudden my dungeon shook, my chains fell off, and glory to God, I cried. My soul was filled. I cried, enough for me—the Saviour died. Now my confidence was strengthened that the Lord, for Christ's sake, had heard my prayers and pardoned all my sins.[1]

The story of black Americans becoming Christians in large numbers begins here. When the Methodist Church was formally organized in 1784 at Lovely Lane Chapel in Baltimore, Richard Allen and Harry Hoosier were there representing one-fifth of the Methodist Church's total membership. By the turn of the century, blacks in the Methodist and Baptist churches were numbered in the tens of thousands. Presbyterians followed at a distant third, and there were smaller numbers of blacks scattered among the other major denominations.

The Black Church Born:
A Response to the American Dilemma

The fervor of the Great Awakening did not resolve the American dilemma. The fire did not burn away the chilling effects of racism, nor did the cool waters of salvation sufficiently chill the burning passions of hate and discrimination. Bigotry seeped through the restraints of faith to join the undertow already sucking at the church's foundations.

For a fleeting moment in American history the church attempted to commit itself to do what the founders of the nation chose not to do; namely, to give *de facto* recognition to the principle that *all* people stand equal before God in their nakedness and need. But it was not to be so. These newly converted black Christians despaired of the peculiar spirituality that confined them to the back pews, the "nigger heavens" and "slave balconies" of white churches. Eventually they walked out to establish their own independent communions.

As one observer put it: "If there had been no racism in America, there would be no racial churches." But there was and there is! And there was a significant group of black Christians who had the grace and spiritual acuity necessary to salvage values from the basic truths that underlay so much dross. They were honest Christians in search of an expression of faith that would transcend the vagaries of human manipulation, whatever their origin. They were determined to be persons of dignity as well as believers in the faith.

40

It was somewhat ironic that these dark descendants of Clement, Origen, Tertullian, Cyprian, Augustine and the other great African intellectuals who worked out the basic political and theological doctrines of the Western church were to have to form new communions. But indeed they did. They developed new worship styles and became the prophets and conscience of the new nation because America had become a place informed by latter-day apostles whose understanding of that faith was clouded by an incipient racism, a degraded economics, a cold formalism, and an illusion of manifest destiny. But neither illumination of the spirit nor the light of reason is a sure hedge to the capriciousness that seems ever the corollary of power, irrespective of race, geography or nationality.

Already, with fear and trembling these black Christians left the white church where they were scorned and demeaned to go to the *other* church, that *invisible institution* which met in the swamps and bayous and the cane breaks to join other black believers in a common experience. Away from the disapproving eyes of the master and beyond the ever-listening ears of the overseer, the shouts that were stifled in their throats like a cork caught in a bottle's neck were released. The agony so long suppressed burdened the air with sobs and screams and rhythmic moans. The ecstasy of unstifled praise and celebration soared without hesitation in glorious adoration to an unchanging God who "builds up Zion walls" and "sets his people free." God's mercy was enjoined; God's justice invoked. And they *had* church! An ex-slave described this invisible institution:

> Our preachers were usually plantation folks just like the rest of us. Some man who had a little education and had been taught something about the Bible would be our preacher. The colored folks had their code of religion, not nearly so complicated as the white man's religion, but more closely observed. . . . When we had our meetings of this kind, *we held them in our own way and were not interfered with by the white folks*. (Italics added.)[2]

A Spiritual Response to the American Dilemma: Birth of the African Churches

The earliest black church was the Baptist Church at Silver Bluffs, South Carolina, established by George Liele in the 1770s. In 1778 Andrew Bryan became pastor of the First African Baptist Church in Savannah, Georgia, succeeding George Liele as leader of what was perhaps the first of the independent black churches. Still there were others to follow in the 1790s. But farther north in Philadelphia something very different happened to change the whole future of the independent black church movement. Evidently, as a result of his preaching, Richard Allen had gathered some forty-two persons around him for prayer and worship in the Free African Society. Organized by him and Absalom Jones in Philadelphia, it was not a church; but, moved by strong evangelical commitment, the society provided an alternative to the pulpits of the religious establishment to which they were denied fully accredited access. Gayraud Wilmore suggests the importance of this society:

> The suitability of the Free African Society pattern for meeting multiple needs in the Black community is amply demonstrated by the rapidity and enthusiasm by which it spread from Philadelphia to other cities. Wherever the Societies were organized they began as protests against white prejudice and neglect and with the objective of providing not only for religious needs, but for social service, mutual aid and solidarity among 'people of African descent.' The African Societies did not only express the need for cultural unity and solidarity, but the protest and resistance of a persecuted people. . . .
>
> It created therefore, the classic pattern for the Black Church in the United States. A pattern of religious commitment that has a double focus—the free and autonomous worship of

God in the way Black people want to worship him, and the unity and social welfare of the Black community.[3]

Since in November of that same year Absalom Jones and Richard Allen, both free men and known for their industry and Christian conduct, were pulled from their knees at St. George's Methodist Episcopal Church, while inadvertently praying in a segregated gallery, the Free African Society turned out to be the forerunner of the first Black Episcopal Church and the African Methodist Episcopal (AME) denominations. St. Thomas, with Absalom Jones as its first pastor, remained within the Episcopal Church, while Bethel A.M.E. (1794) under Allen's leadership later became the mother church of the first black denomination with Allen as its first bishop, established in 1816. The African Methodist Episcopal Zion Church was to follow in 1820, and a series of Baptist and Presbyterian churches were established in New York, Boston, St. Louis and Philadelphia.

In a significant study of this movement, Benjamin Mays and J. W. Nicholson attribute the founding of these and other churches to five characteristic forces: 1) growing racial consciousness, 2) splits and withdrawals, 3) the migration of black people from rural areas in the South to southern and northern cities, 4) individual initiative, and 5) missions started by other churches. These scholars concluded that the black church began "as a means of separating an unwanted racial group from the common public worship,"[4] thereby responding to the American dilemma.

The black Methodists would be joined by yet another Methodist communion, the Christian Methodist Episcopal (CME) Church (1870) [originally "Colored" Methodist Episcopal Church, but changed in 1954 to "Christian"]. The two largest black Baptist churches, the National Baptist Convention, U.S.A. and the National Baptist Convention of America were established in 1880. Within two centuries

43

from the founding of the A.M.E. Church, 95% of black Christians in this country were in separate churches, forming the corpus of black religion in America. Black worship and spirituality developed primarily in these institutions, against the backdrop of the American dilemma.

At the critical junctures of American history the prophetic voices of the churches were muted by a humiliating racism and silenced by the deafening sound of the American dilemma. Black Christians were unwilling to bow to racial idolatry and become a class of spiritual subordinates. Nor were they willing to accept a Christianity that preached, worshipped, and glorified a God who required them to sacrifice their moral and spiritual validity to the "Baal of white supremacy." For them, accepting Christianity did not mean accepting American Christianity. The God they invoked and to whom they had committed themselves transcended the American experience. They relied on their deep, African roots and spiritual experiences; their most reliable counsel was their own theological understanding. And while they were to borrow from the host culture surrounding them—as sign of their unmistakable universal humanity—they were prepared to be borrowed from as well. The result of merging the two diverse influences revealed Africans' ability not only to adapt to new contexts, but to do so creatively.

It was out of this background and in this context that black worship developed. When the Christian faith flowed through the souls of black folk, they reshaped, refashioned, and recreated a style of worship which reflected the cultural and historical background of transplanted Africans in America. Hence a new style of worship from the subculture evolved. But it was neither European nor African; it was a black American style, the essence of soulful worship. This new creation mirrored the tragedy and dreamed a vision of hope for the continuing American dilemma.

IV

The Liturgy of Zion: The Soul of Black Worship

Black Worship and Black Theology

Undoubtedly for as long as African-Americans or black Americans have grappled with the problem of being both Christian and black in a racist society, some form of black Christian theology has existed in America. Somehow, the slaves found a relationship between the God whom they had met in Africa whose sigh was heard in the African wind, and the God of Abraham, Isaac, Jacob and Jesus. And even when white people said one thing about their God, the African heard something else. When the white preacher, as a tool of the slavemaster, stressed the demands of God for the Africans to be slaves, obedient to their masters, the African heard the clear call of a righteous God for justice, equality and freedom.

Much of the black theology is reflected in the religious tradition and worship experience of black people. For it has been their understanding of God through their own black experience that they searched for meaning, relevance, worth, assurance, reconciliation and their proper response to the God revealed. This is what religion is all about; it's where the black worship experience was born. And at any historic point the gathering of the community is central to

45

what happens later and is the support of the souls of black folks.

The Civil Rights Movement of the 1960s was the most telling illustration of the importance of gathering. Hundreds and thousands of people, protesting segregation and discrimination in the South, were willing to face firehoses, police dogs, cattle prods, inhumanly cruel sheriffs, police, and state troopers. Children and adults marched in Selma and St. Augustine, in Birmingham and Montgomery to decry second-class citizenship and segregation. But always before marching they *first* gathered in the church to engage in songs of praise and protest, to entreat the God of history to be their guide, and to hear sermons and testimonies that related the gospel to their unjust social situation, and challenged them to act. The gathering of black folks in worship services reveals the rich culture and the ineffable beauty and creativity of the black soul. Indeed, it intimates the uniqueness of the black religious tradition.

Songs of the Soil and the Soul

The Negro spirituals, which speak of life and death, suffering and sorrow, love and judgment, grace and hope, justice and mercy were born out of this tradition. They were the songs of a people weary at heart. The Negro spirituals were the songs of an unhappy people; and, yet they are the most beautiful expressions of human experience. The music is more ancient than the words. These songs are the siftings of centuries, telling of exile and trouble, of strife and hiding; they grope toward some unseen power and sigh for rest in the end. "But through all the sorrow songs," as William E. B. DuBois pointed out, "there breathes a hope for a faith in the ultimate justice of things."

Gospel songs created in the North became the northern, urban counterparts of the Negro spirituals of the South. The gospel song combines the sheer joy of living with deep religious faith. It arose in the midst of the early exodus from the farms and hamlets of the South when black folks arrived in Chicago, New York, Detroit, and other northern cities, and found themselves in a strange land. The simple lines of the gospel were written on their minds and hearts, and were translated into songs on their lips and praise in their mouths. Now there is little argument that *these* gospel songs and sounds have supplied the roots for much of contemporary music—from rock symphonies to detergent commercials.

Black Worship and White Fundamentalism

Some have argued that there is no difference between black worship and white fundamentalist emotionalism. The answer can be found by experiencing authentic Black worship or attending a Southern white fundamentalist meeting. Clearly, a people's religion and mode of worship derive from the experiences, the physical and psychological realities of their day-to-day existence. Nobody who knows anything about black people and white fundamentalists would argue that their experiences are the same. The white experience in its critical essence is not the black experience.

There is a basic and critical difference between blacks and white fundamentalists as it relates to Scripture. One can search in vain through the official statements of faith, even among black pentecostals, to find references either to "verbal" or "plenary" inspirations of the Bible, which are code words among white fundamentalists. While many blacks can easily be classified as neo-evangelicals who believe in inspiration, they do not generally make statements about inerrancy of Scripture.

This leads to a particular manifestation in preaching and the use of Scripture. Black preachers take much more liberty than do whites with elaborating and the using of imagination in telling biblical stories for the benefit and enjoyment of their listeners. Neither do they make such a fine distinction between the Old and the New Testaments, as if the New superseded the Old. In fact, black preachers tend to preach more often from the Old Testament. And even when they preach from the New Testament the text is more often drawn from the gospels rather than the epistles.[1]

Toward a Definition of Black Worship: The Re-shaping of Worship

Worship, to be authentic, must be the celebration of that which is most real and which serves to sustain life. To be Christian worship, it must necessarily and inevitably relate to the eternal God revealed in Jesus Christ. It involves transcending and deciphering the existential dilemma, discovering the transcendence grounded in being.

Styles and theologies of worship are determined largely by the context in which a people's faith is experienced. Their mode of worship, religious practices, beliefs, rituals, attitudes and symbols are inevitably and inextricably bound to the psychological and physical realities of their day-to-day existence. This is at least part of what William James called "varieties of religious experience." It is quite clear that when the Christian faith flowed through the contours of the souls of black folk a new interpretation, a new form, a new worship style emerged. Reflecting the cultural and historical background of transplanted Africans, it moved with the rhythms of a soulful people and rolled like a prancing river. The black people responded to the Christian faith in their way, not in the way of their oppressor. They reshaped, refashioned, and recreated the Christian religion to meet their own particular needs.

Worship in the black tradition is celebration of the power to survive and to affirm life, with all of its complex and contradictory realities. The secular and the sacred and Saturday night and Sunday morning come together to affirm God's wholeness, the unity of life, and God's lordship over all of life. Such a tradition encourages spontaneity and improvisation, and urges worshippers to turn themselves loose into the hands of the existential here and now, where joy and travail mingle together as part of the reality of God's creation. In this context black people experience and participate in the life and community of faith.

Is Black Worship Distinctive?

"Is black worship distinctive"? Dr. Larry Jones formerly of Union Theological Seminary in New York criticizes this question and is somewhat right but for the wrong reasons. In response to Gayraud Wilmore's questionnaire for the National Committee of Black Churchmen on Black Theology, Dr. Jones makes the following observations:

> It is commonplace where black clergy gather to hear long dissertations on the genius of black worship, but the documentations for the dissertations are more often than not part poetry, part testimony, part exaggeration, part embroided memory and part personal testimony.[2]

In the first place, there is ample documentation for black worship being a product of the black experience and having its own uniqueness and genius. Part of that documentation is in the widespread efforts of some white Christians to add a little "soul" to their styles of worship, creating congregational participation, dialogues, happenings, and celebrations with programmed spontaneity. However, the more dependable documentation is in the souls of black folk who disappear from black churches when services become too stilted, cold, and staid. European-oriented worship services are generally shorter, more rigid in worship form, less emotional. And the music is less spontaneous. Black people go in search of a church where there is some spirit and where exuberant ejaculations of "Thank you, Jesus," "Praise God!" "Preach!" and "Amen!" are not considered to be overreaction of superstitious simple folk or religious revelry. In fact, that is why many black churches, including Union Church in Boston, were separated from white congregations.[3]

In the second place, any serious conversation about worship or anything else that relates to emotional experience is based on "part testimony, part memory and part personal history." In fact, theology as a discipline would be enhanced by personal history and testimony. To say, "This is what happened to me," and to avoid the kind of pervasive gnosticism so current in many systematic theologies is effective and refreshing. Personal testimonies are not irrelevant. In fact, the farther away one is from it, the more imprecise memory's embroidery.

In the third place, every book on worship by white thinkers is based on their experience and understanding of worship in a white context. It reflects the persons' means of transcending and deciphering their existential dilemma. It represents what is most real and sustains life for them.

What are the distinctive elements of black worship? What documentation can be offered for claiming that there is genius in black worship? In James A. Joseph's description of black worship as "Sunday morning gatherings with group psychotherapy and soul music"[4] all that can be said? Is the essence of black worship simply a dramatic ritualization of what Joseph Washington has called "Negro Folk Religion"?

To some extent, the genius of black worship is the same as that which made Shakespeare a literary genius, the ability to create the new and fresh out of the old and stale, to lend a refulgence to the dark and somber, to create a *tertium quid* out of the coming-together of two diverse influences so distinct and different as to be called unique.

This is not to suggest that worship in all black churches has reflected that genius. God alone knows how many times and in how many places black religious gatherings have engaged in "sound and fury signifying nothing." But as we have been willing to recognize the transcendent God in the turmoil of our existential dilemma and to see the "prophetic face of divine anger, undergirded by the Holy Spirit, to bring the sword in pursuit of the positive peace without which no person can experience salvation,"[5] we have participated in the spiritual celebration of life and witnessed the opening up of the "windows of heaven."

Let us look briefly at two aspects of Christian worship in the light of the black experience of faith: ritual and music. The next chapter will focus on preaching.

Ritual: "What Meaneth These Stones?"

In an age when repetition leads to boredom, many see ritual as a bad thing. They equate ritual with formality and see it as something superficial, meaningless, empty, lacking in creativity, cold. A different point of view can be taken for our discussion. Contrary to the arguments of some, ritual is not a bad thing. It allows a people to make a metaphoric statement about the paradoxes and the contradictions of the human situation. Ritual provides an opportunity to connect with others who share the same experience, allowing a recollection of experiences. With rituals people can express their dependency on continuity for their identity and draw upon their memories and the faith of those around them. It is a way of responding to our children's question of, "What meaneth these stones?"

Ritual is not the exclusive property of any particular

group. Ritual and ceremony have always been important to black life and black worship. From the ancient tribal rituals and ceremonies of the Fon-speaking people of Dahomy, the Yoruba of Nigeria and the Akan of Ghana to the grand processionals and recessionals of the multicolored robed choirs, the white starched uniforms of usher boards, and to the grand marches of the masonic and fraternal groups, black people have engaged in ritual. It is an essential part of black life and worship. But a ritual that is meaningful can't be created for all people at all times and places.

Either ritual is rooted in a common culture or it is nothing. And when it ceases to be relevant to the lives of the people, it is no longer useful. Genuine religious ritual has to be accessible to the unsophisticated and naive as well as the informed and liturgical. James Russell Lowell was right:

New occasions teach new duties.
Time makes ancient good uncouth.

Ritual must fit the time and the place. One can say about ritual what Merton said about church architecture:

(People) build churches as if a church should not belong to our time. A church has to look as if it were left over from some other age. I think such an assumption is based on an implicit confession of atheism as if God did not belong to all ages.[6]

God does belong to all ages, and ritual used in black worship ought to reflect the meaning of life in relation to God and what God is doing about the experience of living as black people in this world. To be meaningful in black worship, ritual must speak to the needs of black folk and must reflect their problems, affirm their worth in the sight of God and inspire them militantly to seek the solutions to their problems. Rites, ceremonies, and liturgies, like theology, cannot be developed in isolation from the crucial problems of a people's survival. Ritual ought to affirm the liberating presence of God in our human experience. As Major Jones has rightly put it, "God is not on our side: we are on His side if we are for liberation." And that ought to be reflected in liturgies and rituals.

Ritual loses its effectiveness when it alienates a people from their heritage, their society and their family. Carlton W. Molette, author of *Afro-American Studies*, has pointed out that there are different purposes for Afro-American ritual drama than the traditional purposes of modern Euro-American ritual drama. Using the Afro-American church service as the model, since it is the most widely supported ritual drama in the black community, Molette delineates the difference in purpose.

One of these purposes is *to celebrate the affirmation of a sense of community, a feeling of togetherness.* This is sometimes emphasized through ritual mass physical contact, such as joining hands or touching in some way, so that spiritual togetherness is reaffirmed and heightened by a ritual form of physical togetherness. The accent is on *community* rather than on the individual, *fellowship* rather than individual uniqueness.

A second purpose, according to Molette, is *to serve some functional, useful purpose.* The ritual drama is expected to have some future effect outside of the framework of the ritual itself. This can be illustrated by the funeral ritual in which the soul of the deceased is expected to be affected by the ritual itself.

A third purpose of the ritual drama is *to create a spiritual involvement (or emotional involvement) in the event.* This is designed to provide a purgation of the emotions. The church service is expected to allow all to be emotionally and spiritually involved.

When these purposes are met in the worship service, black people are apt to say: "We *had* church today!"

Molette's analysis is instructive. The ritual that does not take into account this cultural heritage and does not relate to the emotional, day-to-day existence of black people is seen as meaningless. Liturgy ought to reflect and relate to everyday life as black Christians struggle to make sense of life, and worship ought to reflect a captive and alienated people in a strange land, a people in pursuit of liberation, freedom, health, and wholeness. Part of this change may mean making use of poetry and other works developed in the First and Second Renaissance of Black Culture and the poetry and literary works being developed by young black prophets today.

This is not to suggest change in ritual as a vogue. Fads come and go. And God knows that the black community knows that well. But there is a difference between faddism and change. Change is the natural evolution, but faddism is artificial. Faddism seeks change simply for change's sake and may lack taste, judgment and sensitivity. We want change for liberation's sake. We want change for God's sake; and we make the rituals we use relevant to the people's lives and to their struggle to survive, to be liberated, and to celebrate.

Let's find new and interesting ways to praise the Lord. Some will accuse us of having an aspect of entertainment about it and worship in the black tradition *is* art. It is *drama*, as Molette points out. The black experience is one where a person dramatizes. Let our rituals reflect a people in pursuit of their liberation and what God means in that struggle and celebrate the wholeness found.

Music: Is There a Song?

Music in the black worship tradition is as close to worship as breathing is to life. It has been the songs of Zion in this strange land that have often kept black folks from "starting down the steep and slippery steps of death" in suicide. These songs have cut a path through the wilderness of despair.

There is no one more eminently qualified to comment on the spirituals than John Wesley Work, who was for many years professor of Latin and history at Fisk University and one of the pioneers in collecting, arranging and presenting the Negro spirituals. He says in his book, *Folk Songs of the American Negro:*

> To our fathers who came out of bondage and who are still with us, these songs are prayers, praises and sermons. They sang them at work; in leisure moments; they crooned them to their babies in the cradles; to their wayward children; they sang them to their sick, wracked with pain on beds of affliction; they sang them over their dead. Blessings, warnings, benedictions and the very heartbeats of life were all expressed to our fathers by their song.

These songs of hope and promise have helped to bring a people through the torture chambers of the last two centuries.

The music of the black religious tradition has said that just being alive is good and worth celebrating, singing, and shouting about. It is impossible to conceive of the black religious tradition in any authentic sense without the songs of survival, liberation, hope, and celebration. That music has nourished the black community, soothed its hurts, sustained its hopes, and bound its wounds. It has proclaimed that God whom we knew in the forests of Africa, the Lord whose voice was heard in the sighing of the night wind, the God whom we met in the cotton field of the Southland is the joy of our salvation. It is that God who makes us glad to come into the house of the Lord. The music of the black religious tradition has enabled a people to keep on going, to keep on tramping. Black music lifts the heads, hearts, and spirits of the congregation in readiness to hear the gospel word of grace and liberation.

The role music plays in black worship has its antecedents in Western Africa, where most black slaves came from. Black worship in America recreates patterns which have been observed in East African religious practices. Music in ritual in both cultures is of dominant importance. LeRoi Jones (Imamu Baraka) quotes in *Blues People* an old African dictum which says, "The spirit will not descend without song." In Africa, ritual dances and songs were integral parts of African religious observances. This heritage of emotional religion was one of the strongest contributions that the African culture made to the Afro-American. The puritan Christian church by and large saw dancing as an evil, worldly excess, but dancing as an integral part of the African's life could not be displaced by the still white notes of the Wesleyan hymnal.

From the earliest times when the black slaves sang:

Oh, freedom! Oh, freedom all over me! When I am free! An' befor' I'd be a slave, I'll be buried in my grave, an' go home to my Lord an' be free. (#102)

until the singing of

Go down, Moses, way down in Egypt land, Tell ole Pharaoh, to let my people go, (#112)

black people were not *simply* singing a song, they were expressing *a definite point of view*. That point of view was that the God of justice and the God of Jesus is on the side of the oppressed. This was and is at the heart of black religion in America. And it must be reaffirmed in our worship experiences and taught to our children. We must not neglect our past, our roots. Our children must be made aware that "we have come over a way that with tears has been

56

watered'' (#32 and #210); that we have sung the songs of freedom and liberation and hope—even when ''hope unborn had died.''

Some have argued that the gospel songs that originated primarily in the North, and are popular throughout the states, border on the secular. The gospel songs are characterized by the beat, rhythm and group vibrations. Some have maintained that the lyrics are banal. The truth is that the songs talk about the things that matter most to poor people. When you are well off, you can write songs about individual neuroses. But poor people struggling to survive—whether in rat-infested ghetto flats or on a sharecropper's farm in Mississippi—are concerned about staying alive. They can sing and mean, ''It's another day's journey and I'm glad about it!''

As to whether gospel songs are secular, a statement made by the late Duke Ellington at a 1965 Christmas program at Fifth Avenue Presbyterian Church in New York City is helpful. The Duke was speaking to the question of ''What makes music sacred?'' He said:

> Sacred music in all of its forms offers a universal point of meeting. But what makes music sacred is not a rigid category nor a fixed pattern of taste. The sole criterion is whether or not the hearts of the musician and the listener are offered in response and devotion to God.[7]

While the Duke was not a prince of the church, his statement is sufficiently sound for all of us. The black religious tradition understands that the rational and the emotional go together. Life is emotional as well as rational. The late Howard Thurman, Dean of Marsh Chapel, Boston University for many years, used to say: ''The mind is the latest addition to man's equipment, and when you minister to him on the assumption that he is mind only, you are a fool.'' The black religious tradition in its authenticity is not

57

that foolish; it erases the line between mind and body, intellect and emotion, and ministers to the rationality and emotionality of the whole person. It is this gift of faith that God has given us through the black experience. We must boldly offer it on the altars of the church without fear and without shame.

If Luther's "A Mighty Fortress Is Our God" can raise the blood pressure of Lutherans, and if the sons and the daughters of the founders of the American church can be stirred to tears in the singing of the Quaker hymn, "Dear Lord and Father of Mankind," and if James Russell Lowell's hymn can make thunder roll for the sons and daughters of the New England abolitionists and the vanguards of white liberals, then Thomas Dorsey's "Precious Lord, Take My Hand" ought to be able to make lightning flash in black congregations—even those held in bourgeois captivity. And Charles Tindley's "We'll Understand It Better By and By" (#55) ought to raise spiritual tumult in any black Methodist Church.[8]

Even with the hymns of the church, and especially those about the unearned and the unmerited grace of God, black folks are not always singing the same song the white folks are singing. A hymn like "Amazing Grace"—even though written by an ex-slave trader—becomes a song of survival and liberation in a different cadence and sound. It becomes a new song. For what black people sing about is the miracle of their survival. Imamu Baraka (LeRoi Jones) has quite rightly observed:

> The God spoken about in black songs is not the same one in white songs. Though the words might look the same. (They are not even pronounced alike.) But it is a different quality of energy they summon.[9]

V

Black Preaching and Its Message: "Is There Any Word From the Lord?"

Black Preaching and Black Theology

Contrary to the thought of some, black theology may be first and foremost found in the folklore and literature of the black church; and in the pronouncement, philosophy, of the spokepersons of the black church. That is, black preaching may be the major source of black theology. It is the preached word that contains the content of black people's thought in an effort to appropriate the Christian faith in a racist white society in America.

Through the insight of the black preacher, the transplanted African saw a relationship between the God whom he or she had known in the African forest; (whose existence was affirmed in African proverbs, songs, prayers, myths, and religious ceremonies) and the God of Abraham, Isaac and Jacob whom the white preacher talked about in America.[1]

And even when the white preacher tried to convince the African slave that the God of the Bible is a God who requires the slaves to be obedient to their masters and subservient to the white people, the slaves heard the call of God for justice, equality and freedom. No wonder they responded: "Befor' I'd be a slave, I'll be buried in my

59

grave, an' go home to my Lord an' be free.'' (#102) The God of the Bantu and the Ashanti, the God of the Zulu and the Fanti is also the God of Abraham, Isaac and Jacob, Jesus, Malcolm and Martin and that God has been seen by the Black preacher as the same God who commanded Moses to tell Pharaoh to let God's people go. This the slave preacher understood and when the house slaves did not, the field hands were ready to ''steal away to Jesus'' (#134) and on to the brush arbor to the liberation rally.

The journey from slavery to freedom, from bondage to emancipation was made more bearable by the role that the black preacher played. It was the black preacher who stood midway between the inexhaustible storehouse of spiritual dynamics and the depleted lives of black brothers and sisters and shouted: ''Walk together, children, don't you get weary.'' (#156) And sometimes it was the black preacher who moaned to a bewildered and beleaguered flock: ''There is a balm in Gilead'' (#123) as they traced the rainbow through the rain.

The Black Preacher as Leader

This preacher has been the natural leader of the black community. His or her art has been charismatic preaching. The preacher's tool has been what somebody called ''the sledgehammer of truth.'' From Harry Hosier, who travelled with Bishop Asbury, to Malcolm and Martin, and the unnamed ''sons of thunder,'' God has taken the sometimes stammering and stuttering words of otherwise prosaic preachers and made them the power instrument by which a people survived the torture chambers of the last two centuries in this nation. They provided hope in a time when all seemed futile. Preachers gave people the will to keep on going when suffering seemed endless.

Black preaching is both a product of the black church and

a powerful force around which the black church has been organized. It has sustained a suffering people; it has soothed their hurts, bound their wounds, and provided "angles of vision" for a despairing and desperate people. It has provided the hope without which a people would have been destroyed. But while black preaching is a product and a force of the black church, its mode, its style, its rhetoric and its form have extended beyond the church and into all parts of the black community.

The style and pattern of black preaching can be heard from the speeches of politicians, to the rap of young people on the streets, to the community meetings of black folk. This is significant in the black community where the spoken word, the rhetoric and the oral tradition are so vastly important. Perhaps it is the language of oppression, the rhetorical style of a people whose daily existence is threatened by the insidious tentacles of white power and oppression, but whose affirmation of life is strong nevertheless.

The Role of Black Preaching in Worship

As it has been to all of Christianity, preaching is central in authentic black worship. The proclamation of the Word of God, telling of the story, is essential to authentic black worship.

It is interesting to note the Pentecost event: it was not the speaking in tongues, as fiery as they were. It was not that men and women had gathered from every nation under the heaven, as international and impressive as that was. Pentecost reached its climax only after someone stood up and preached with the passion of one who had been in touch with the living Christ! People began to ask, "What shall we do?" Three thousand souls were added to the church only after the Word was preached.

Preaching is central in the black church. There is a saying

among some of the brothers and sisters of the cloth that people will forgive you for anything but *not preaching*. Black folk expect the preacher to tell the story. They expect an answer to Jeremiah's question: "Is there any word from the Lord?" (Jeremiah 37:17) And they have subtle and not-so-subtle ways of letting the preacher know when that Word is not forthcoming.

Black Preaching Characterized

What we must do now is to characterize the art and the unique style of black preaching in the black church tradition, comment on its characteristics, illustrate a few points, and offer some encouragement of the tradition.

1. *Black preaching, almost without exception, is biblical.* It weaves the biblical message and stories so that they come alive and affect the life experiences of the congregation. Stories like "The Eagle Stirs Her Nest," "Your Bed Too Short and Your Cover Too Narrow," "Dry Bones," and "Jonah" are favorites that can be used to describe black Americans in white denominations. Black United Methodists are like Jonah, and the large, powerful denomination like the whale. The whale cannot digest them and it cannot spew them out. From the "Good Samaritan" parable, black folk are compared to the man from Jericho who fell among thieves. Black folk have fallen among thieves who have stolen their names, their heritage, their rights, their religion, and their culture; thieves who threaten to rob them of their humanity, their dreams and souls. The unconnected, dry bones story from Ezekiel reflects what is happening in the black community with various programs, movements, community organizations, and efforts of liberation to connect the black community.

Now each of these stories can be told in such a way that it does not violate the biblical story but develops relevance for black folk. The point to be made is that black preaching is basically, and almost without exception, biblical. While some white middle-class Protestant churches suffer through small homilies on small subjects, lectures and advice on "how to use your leisure time" and other such mundane subjects in search of relevancy, the black church finds poignancy, relevance and a continually guiding Word from the Old Book.

Black preaching is rich with passionate words and vivid imagery for a disillusioned and disinherited people. It tells the "old, old story" which sets hearts aflame and spirits right. The stories help solidify a faith that God is more than a match for evil structures of oppression, and God supremely illustrates that power to overcome at Calvary. We are reminded over and over again that in spite of what happens on Capitol Hill there is a higher hill—Calvary.

2. *Black preaching is characterized generally as prophetic rather than pastoral.* More often than not the Old Testament and the prophetic literature are used as material for sermonizing and as the basis of the text rather than the more pastoral material of the Bible. One can add the synoptic Gospel tradition to that since the synoptic Gospels of Matthew, Mark and Luke are the testimonies of those witnesses who knew the prophet Jesus and his revolutionary activities in and around Galilee as he struggled with the powerful Roman government and the religious establishment of his day.

A survey of sermons preached on the September Sunday morning on which the four black children were bombed to death at Sixteenth Street Baptist Church in Birmingham, Alabama, revealed that almost without exception, the black preachers preached from the Old Testament. The white preachers, almost without exception, preached from the New Testament. This was not a coincidence. Black preaching tends to announce judgment on the nation, and to call prophetically into question the responsible institutions in society; white preaching tends to be of a pastoral nature.

Part of the reason for this is that the American white

church has a different relationship to the establishment than the black church. When Christianity is so inextricably bound to Americanism and the ''American way of life,'' it sees God, country, and the American flag as almost synonymous terms. The emphasis more often than not in preaching from this perspective is on personal behavior and the individual rather than the revolutionary ethic of Jesus and the prophetic judgment on the whole community. Sheer morality gets confused with the demands of the gospel. One can be highly moral and not be Christian.

A second difference here is that there is not the strict dichotomy in the black tradition of the priestly and the prophetic, the sacred and the secular. The priestly and the prophetic co-exist as part and parcel of the same reality. And even where there is clear judgment and the prophetic message, the celebration of life is always present.

3. *Generally, black preaching is poetic rather than rigorously logical and stymied by rationality.* As Hortense Spillers has pointed out in her analysis of the style of the black sermon in reference to Martin Luther King, there is considerable use of metaphors and nominality with a greater number of nouns, adjectives and adjectival clauses rather than verbs and verb forms.[2] These combine to create a picturesqueness and grandness of speech.

The black preacher relies on imagery to carry the subject much like the language of the Bible. This can be illustrated from a sermon preached by Dr. J. H. Jackson, President of the National Baptist Convention, in 1962. In this sermon an effort is made to paint a picture on the mind's canvas. Jackson is addressing himself to facing the future with God:

> But I say to you my friends, fear not your tomorrow, and shirk not from the task or the lot that is yet to come. The future belongs to God, and the last chapter in the story of human life will not be written by the blood-stained hands of godless men but by the God of history himself. The same

hand that raised the curtain of creation and pushed back the floating worlds upon the broad sea of time and flashed forth the light of life that put an end to ancient chaos and darkness; the same hand that erected the highways of the skies and rolled the sun like a golden ball across the pavement of the dawn; the same God whose hand has guided the destinies of nations, fixed the time and seasons and superintended the whole order of time and eternity will at His appointed hour pull down the curtain of existence, and will Himself write the last paragraph in the last chapter of the last book of human life and cosmic destiny.[3]

Such poetry, vivid imagery, and word pictures can be heard again and again in black preaching in almost any North American city, town or hamlet.

What Warner Traynam says about black theology can be said about black preaching (and if it is accepted what has been suggested at the start, to some extent, we are talking about the same thing when we speak of black preaching and black theology). The question is not "Is there a God?" (a philosophical and rational question), but is "Who is God? What does God's existence mean for me? What does the Lord say about my condition?" The black preacher is clear that liberation and salvation are not accomplished by philosophical debate and rational argument. The black preacher makes an effort to communicate with both the mind and the emotions.

4. *Black preaching is dialogical, i.e., a cooperative effort between the pulpit and the pew.* The dialogue does not take place *after* the sermon but rather *during* the sermon. Sometimes a mediocre and unpoetical preacher can achieve lyrical power when there is *cooperation from the pew*: the support and expectancy, and the encouragement and enthusiasm of the congregation. In such instances, a "son of man" becomes a "son of thunder." Or as one of these unknown "sons of thunder" put it: "He explained the unexplainable, defined the undefinable, pondered the imponderable, and unscrewed the inscrutible."

Part of the black preaching tradition has been the prayers of the lay people for the preacher and/or the expectancy about the sermon. (For example, read James Weldon Johnson's prayer "Listen Lord," in *God's Trombones*, Penguin Books, Viking Press.)[4] These prayers reflect the same vivid imagery, poetry, and imagination mentioned earlier. With such help as that from the pew and the expectancy from the congregation, a black shepherd spoke with power to a bewildered flock. But always the black preacher is aware that he or she is on the most important errand that God commissions.

There was an old lady named Aunt Bea in Haven Church in Anniston, Alabama. Aunt Bea must have been at least eighty. The preacher had just finished seminary and was convinced that he had the best theological degree in the nation. But as he strained and struggled to make the gospel clear, preaching with all of the power and passion and persuasion he could muster, Aunt Bea strained and struggled with him. When he was in the throes of a point and trying to get it across, one could hear Aunt Bea, once in a while say, "Jes' hep' him, Jesus!" She was always with him, a part of the cooperative effort of preaching. She knew that preaching in the black tradition was a matter of cooperation between the pulpit and the pew. That is the black style of dialogical preaching whose roots reach back into the wombs of Africa. It is call-and-respond style and the participation of all those gathered makes black preaching the unique and beautiful art that it is.

5. *Black preaching is didactic as well as inspiring.* It seeks to inform as well as inspire. It seeks to discern the action of God in history as it relates to the existential dilemma of those gathered. It seeks to speak to the human condition, to lend healing to hurting souls, to bring a "balm of Gilead" to the tortured spirits of the folks, and to proclaim a liberating and healing word. But, it does not deny the reality of pain.

Some have accused black preaching and the black church of anti-intellectualism. What is more accurate is that there is little tolerance for rarefied abstractions. The black preacher can discuss anything of philosophical and theological import as long as it can be presented in such a way as to make sense of life and relate to the lives of the hearers. How an issue is presented is often more important than what the issue is. People such as Gardner C. Taylor, Howard Thurman, George Outen, Vernon John and Martin Luther King, Jr., Leontine Kelly and Joseph Lowery have proven that black preaching can contain intricate historical-political analyses while at the same time "feeding the flock."

6. *Black preaching is characterized as matter of fact; it is declarative rather than suggestive.* Somebody has said that when the Roman Catholic priests speak, they say, "The church says . . ." When the Jewish rabbis speak, they say, "The Torah says . . ." But when the black preachers speak they say, "This is the Word from the Lord." They tend to drop the plumb line. For example their sermons do not try to show the strengths and weaknesses of the arguments for or against a corrupted president. Rather, their approach would be "Lay the axe to the tree."

There is little room in black preaching for equivocation and spurious sophistry. The moral issues of the nation are far too clear; the presence of evil is too certain to be tentative. A stand is taken on an issue. And even when logical argument is used to present the case, the force of the preaching does not depend on argument and logical persuasion, but rather on the ability of the black preacher to probe the depths of the issue, to guide the hearers to reach the same conclusion. But always it is declarative rather than suggestive, matter of fact rather than tentative. The black preacher is neither timid nor hesitant to say, "Thus saith the Lord!"

7. *Black preaching is characterized as slow and deliberate to a build-up.* The path the preacher takes may be

winding with a few detours, but always he or she is expected to be heading someplace and to take time getting there. In fact, in many congregations, the black preacher can hear some of the congregation admonishing, "Take your time." The preacher is expected to allow time for both the mind and the emotions to react in a natural process reaction. The black preacher is deliberate with the material and nobody has the sense that the preacher is in a hurry, for there is no place more important, and nothing more significant than what they are doing—answering Jeremiah's question, *offering a Word from the Lord.*

It is at this point that many seminaries and particularly homiletics departments have engaged in what Gilbert Caldwell calls "arrogance." The emphasis is on introducing a number of concepts rather than reaching the *feelings* as well as the *minds* of the congregation. *The black preacher is clear to say fewer things and be heard and felt than to present many ideas that are merely words and concepts introduced.*

Many contemporary teachers of homiletics such as Fred Craddock, Eugene Lowry, David Buttrick, Laurence Stookey and others have discovered this secret, and are sharing it with their students. But Zan Holmes, a black professor of preaching at Perkins School of Theology, has always known, taught and practiced this: that the old black preacher in Alabama offered good and sound advice in his dictum:

Start low; go slow,
Go high; strike fire.
Sit down.

8. *The dramatic pause by many preachers is used both as an effort to force the congregation to anticipate what is to follow and to reflect upon what has been said.* This leads to the kind of antiphonal response and sometimes into a

kind of rhythmic, harmonious sing-song. One can describe this pattern as the four r's: rhetoric, repetition, rhythm and rest. This was heard often in the preaching of Martin Luther King, Jr. and thousands of other black preachers. Often it is the repetition of a single word or phrase in which the congregation picks up the cadence of the preacher and there is almost a refrain. Recall King's speech at the Lincoln Memorial in Washington in 1963 in which there is repeated, "I have a dream . . ." By repetition and amplification, the speech builds. There is rhetoric, repetition, rhythm and rest. The congregation (audience) echoes and verifies the preacher's own words in such a way as to make them emphatic.

King was familiar with this technique for he had learned it from his elders and had seen its effect time and time again. He was a virtual master at euphony, i.e., using pleasant sounds with combination of vowels and consonants so as to make pleasing and pleasant, almost sweet sounds. He relied on his sense of euphony and resonance, more than gesture and movement to get his message across. One almost needs to hear this to understand it; for the most effective observer of this style and technique is the human ear.

9. *Black preaching is expected to relate to life and the life situations of the congregation.* When it does not, no matter how well-conceived or how well-constructed or how theologically sound, that sermon is considered a failure. Illustrations are often used—drawn from history, everyday experiences, black history, folk culture and literature, or the biblical literature—and embellished in such a way as to relate the experience to the lives of as many persons as possible.

10. *There is always an element of hope and optimism in black preaching.* No matter how dark a picture has been painted or how gloomy, there is always a "but" or a

"nevertheless" or an element in the climax of the sermon that suggests holding on, marching forward, going through, or overcoming.

A Plea for Preaching: "There Is a Word from the Lord"

As important as ritual is to try to symbolize the acts of the faith and our experience with God; as important as music is to convey the gospel of hope and the beauty of God's holiness, in the Christian religion these can never be *substitutes* for the proclamation of the Word of God. The people of God gather to hear a Word from the Lord. They expect there to be a Word in season and out of season. They want to "hear from on high." They come seeking bread as weary, hungry travellers and deserve to be fed, not just the bread from the oven or simply the bread of the Word, but the Bread of Life.

Jesus did not neglect the blind and the lame, the deaf and the lepers, the poor and the broken-hearted, the captive and the bruised. His gospel of liberation and love and freedom was a declaration of the rule of God breaking in like light upon the forces that hold humans captive. Jesus did not separate a gospel of change of conditions in society from a change of the individual. His gospel is always, and at the same time, *personal and social.* He knew nothing of a religion that spoke to the heart and not the conditions in which men and women lived. But Christ's words in Matthew 10 are clear: "As you go, preach!"

Our prayers and songs, our preaching and liturgy, our symbolic and ritual action must reflect a people who, while they were in captivity, had pursued liberation, freedom, health and wholeness. In that pursuit we found and continue to find a great Savior, Jesus Christ, the Emancipator who sets us all free. As Paul says, and many others testify: "Whom He makes free is free indeed."

My plea is that we preach the Word with power and passion, using the tools of the spirit and the scythe of the gospel to cut a path through the wilderness of the despair. My desire is that we lend healing to the hurting souls of our people, bring the Balm of Gilead to the torturous convulsion of spirits of those who are bruised, hurt, underloved, confused, despairing. We should proclaim the liberating gospel and the healing word of Christ's affliction for the sake of *his whole body*. Perhaps we are called by God in the aeon of the decline of humanity to bring a healthy and healing word to a sick church and a sick society—to set at liberty both the *captors* and the *captives* with the freeing Word, that God in Jesus Christ is our Liberator.

VI

The Songs of Zion *in the Liturgy of Zion*

Songs of Zion has proven that the musical genres in worship in any Christian church can be broadened. Its wide use in diverse places has made a valuable contribution to the enrichment of worship—sometimes unsuspectingly. These songs of the soul have helped strangers and pilgrim people to celebrate on the journey. While many of the songs reflect a past of slavery and servitude and the struggle for freedom and liberation, others focus on the present with its continuing demands and perplexities, providing spiritual strength and moral stamina for facing these realities, and an ever-present hope for a future that will reflect the rulership of God over the principalities and powers.

The Variety of Songs of Zion

The *Songs of Zion* songbook is a pluralistic collection revealing the diversity of the black religious worship traditions and the multifaceted black experience in America. This fact shows itself in the variety of themes and genres utilized to musically express the faith.

73

Negro Spirituals

The Negro spirituals are songs which speak of life and death, suffering and sorrow, love and judgment, grace and hope, justice and mercy, redemption and reconciliation. But, the spirituals are not one. They vary in melody, form, scales and texture. The melodic variety, for example, can be seen by classifying them into three groups: (1) the "call-and-response" chant involving a leader making a short melodic statement and the congregation responding to the statement made by the leader ("Great Day," #142); (2) the syncopated, segmented melody in which the musical line is often made up of short segments with a syncopated figure instead of a complete, sustained phrase, and usually the tempo is fast ("Every Time I Feel the Spirit," #121); and (3) the slow, sustained long phrase melody in which the tempo is slow and the phrase line long and sustained ("My Lord! What a Mourning," #145).

The spirituals not only differ in themes and texts, but there is a great variety in melody and tempo. They provide our congregations and choirs with a variety of religious experiences and expressions and avoid stereotyping the Negro spirituals. These songs were selected and designed to avoid the misconceptions, held in the past by so many, that the spirituals were merely slow, plaintive "sorrow songs" to the neglect of the celebrative jubilee songs. The spirituals provided an opportunity for a variety of emotional expressions. Many, if not most, of our congregations need a chance to express some improvisation and spontaneity. The spirituals provide the opportunity.

Negro Spirituals and the Old Testament

The Old Testament was used extensively in the texts of the Negro spirituals. In an age when the Old Testament has been so vastly neglected in our worship and preaching (except for the Psalms and selected writings from Isaiah), and with the growing use of the common lectionary, the Negro spirituals add much balance and continuity to our worship. They defy the misconceived dichotomy of the Old Testament as law and the New Testament as grace still so prevalent in many Protestant churches.

While telling the stories of the Hebrews, the Negro spirituals find the "grace notes" in the Old Testament over and over again, helping us to avoid the old heresy that the New Testament cancelled out the Old Testament. The spirituals re-enforce the substantial theological truth that God does draw straight with crooked lines, and that God's acts of revelation and relation to the created are gracious.

Hymns

The hymn is our standard musical genre for congregational singing. The promotion and encouragement of congregational hymn singing is one of Methodism's most valuable and lasting contributions to Christian worship. It is no surprise then that Charles Albert Tindley, a black Methodist preacher, turned poet religious song writer, would use the hymn as his medium. But his gospel hymns comprised an entirely new genre as he allowed the Negro spirituals to heavily influence the works he produced. Incorporating proverbs, folk images, biblical allusions well-known to black Christians, he had considerable influence on black hymnody and a universal appeal to the human heart with words of hope, grace, love and pity. One of his hymns, "When the Storms of Life are Raging," is the only hymn by a black composer included in the former Methodist *Book of Hymns*. Perhaps the committee did not know of his more than 40 other hymns. Perhaps they did not know of other black hymn writers and their songs. We are more fortunate now to have a greater number included in the new *United Methodist Hymnal*.

Other black hymn writers include Dr. and Mrs. William Townsend, E. W. D. Isaac, Lucie E. Campbell and others. Their songs, although not necessarily called "hymns" at the time, were issued in several National Baptist Convention publications: *Carols of Glory, Gospel Pearls, Awakening Echoes* and *The Baptist Standard Hymnal*, and were the possessions of scores of soloists, choirs and appropriately found on the piano and in the piano bench of many families. In fact, many young fledgling piano students learned some of these as their first religious compositions to be performed on Sunday evenings at church. Dr. Don Lee White, in his study of black hymnody of this period, has revealed hundreds of such songs.

It is a lasting credit to Methodism that the refrain of Tindley's hymn, "I'll Overcome Sunday," was picked up and transformed into the greatest of freedom songs during the Civil Rights movement. "We Shall Overcome" is sung today, not only by Americans who struggle to finish resolving the American dilemma; it is sung by Nicaraguans who struggle for freedom, by Polish workers who seek justice, the East Germans in their search and stride toward freedom, the South Africans as they resist apartheid, and literally hundreds of thousands of others around the world who seek to overcome oppression and deprivation.

There are other popular Tindley gospel hymns used by blacks and others of all denominations because of their strong universal appeal. Dr. J. Jefferson Cleveland reminded us that Tindley "bequeathed to all Methodism and to Christianity a legacy that will live on through his hymns." One way of accepting that gift to strengthen and enrich our worship experience was to include twelve of his hymns from *Songs of Zion*.

It is interesting to note in the Tindley hymns (and usually missing in other hymns) an emphasis on aging. It is present in "When the Storms of Life Are Raging," but also in other Tindley hymns (e.g., "Leave It There," #23).

Black hymn writing, however, did not begin or end with Tindley. Several other hymns composed by contemporary black writers are included in *Songs of Zion*. One of the most widely sung and greatly appreciated in this group is C. Eric Lincoln's "A Prayer for Love" (#70), which combines the themes of peace and justice, and James Weldon Johnson's "Lift Every Voice and Sing," affectionately called "The Negro National Anthem," or "The Black National Anthem."

One of the advantages of including a few traditional hymns in *Songs of Zion* is that certain arrangements reflect an improvisation of melodies. Harmonies and rhythms are changed to reflect the black worship experience but can easily be used by all.

Gospel Songs

The gospel song comes into existence as the northern urban version of the southern rural Negro spiritual. It shows the influence of the Negro spiritual, the Tindley era of gospel hymns, jazz and blues. Originally called "gospels" because the themes were based on the life of Jesus as recorded in the Gospels in the New Testament, the gospel song has evolved and continues to evolve in our time and contemporary society. Tindley's influence on Thomas A. Dorsey is essentially the beginning of this musical genre. Dorsey's "Precious Lord, Take My Hand" signals the popularity and influence of gospel songs. This song combines intense religious devotion and reaction to realism. It is almost standard in all black churches to sing this song at funerals (which still usually are conducted in the church building, and not in a funeral home). It is used often and variously and would be known by most every black Christian.

Many of these hymns are not original in music, but original in text. In fact, Thomas Dorsey's famous

"Precious Lord" is very similar to "Must Jesus Bear the Cross Alone?" This was not a theft of the compositions of others. As was the case in the oral tradition, and later even with John Wesley and some of his tracts (including his famous one against slavery), "borrowing" was common. The dictum was: *One was free to borrow as long as the revision made the borrowed music better.* Anybody who ever heard Mahalia Jackson, Aretha Franklin or scores of other blacks perform "Precious Lord" knows one certainly does not hear "Must Jesus Bear." One *really* hears "Precious Lord."

But the gospel song, like the Negro spiritual, is varied and diverse and ranges from the slow, moving, plaintive and mournful to the almost jazz-like, with many stops and steps and blue notes in between. Usually it divides into three categories (but exists in parallel fashion): (1) *Historic*—including composers such as Thomas Dorsey, Kenneth Morris, Roberta Martin, Lucie Campbell, etc. "Precious Lord, Take My Hand" (#179) and "Let It Breathe on Me" (#244); (2) *Modern*—which begins at the end of the 1950s and later shows the influence of radical social change and the period symbolized by Martin Luther King Jr.'s leadership "Give Me a Clean Heart" (#182) and "We've Come This Far by Faith" (#192); and (3) *Contemporary*—showing the development and influence of jazz and more technically developed instruments, as well as more sophisticated and complex rhythms and forms "Move Me" (#185), and the various Hawkins' compositions, and Andrae Crouch's "Soon and Very Soon" (#198).

The influence of the black gospel song has clearly influenced and continues to influence our taste in music in every area and informs our musical expectations. Nowhere is this more apparent than in the music of young people of every color or religious denomination. It is also clearly seen in the so-called "white gospel," especially among the evangelicals and young church musicians.

VII

Songs of Zion
and Liturgical Time

Certain Sundays do fall within two complexes of time: the Lenten-Easter complex, and the Advent-Christmas complex, which together cover about one half of the calendar year.

Easter

Easter is not simply a day but a season which begins and ends on Sundays; *Easter Day* is the inauguration of which Pentecost is the culmination. It is usually referred to as the "Great Fifty Days" to indicate its festival nature. The following are appropriate for use throughout the season:

6—"Easter People, Raise Your Voices"
30—"He Lives"
168—"He Arose"
233—"He is Lord"

Easter Day (First Sunday of Easter)
The theme is the proclamation of the resurrection of the Lord, as revealed in his appearance to his followers, particularly to the women who came to the tomb. All this is seen as the New Testament corollary to the Exodus; for as Moses brought the people out of slavery to Pharaoh through

79

the waters of the sea, so Christ has brought us out of slavery to sin and death through the waters of baptism.

Two hymns rarely associated with this day but quite appropriate to it are (1) "In the Garden" (#44), intended to be a song of Mary Magdalene to Jesus in the garden near to the tomb on Easter morning. (2) "Go Down, Moses" (#112 and 212) admirably fitting the Old Testament lectionary account (Exodus 14:10-15) for the first service (Vigil) of Easter Day.

Second Sunday of Easter ("Thomas Sunday")

In all three years of the lectionary, the gospel reading reports Jesus' appearance to Thomas a week after the resurrection (John 20). While few hymns or songs deal directly with this story, the following are appropriate to the theme of the need of Thomas and the grace of Christ: "Let Jesus Fix It for You" (#47) and "Come Here Jesus, If You Please" (#236).

Third Sunday of Easter ("Meal Sunday")

In Year A, the Gospel reading centers on Jesus' revelation of himself in the journey of Emmaus and the breaking of the bread with his followers (Luke 24:13-35). The centrality of Easter Day indicates that the Christian faith rests on the conviction that Christ is raised from the dead. Because of the importance of this annual observance, Easter Day is surrounded by major worship occasions.

The Great Fifty Days

As the Feast of Passover among the Jews inaugurated a festival time of seven weeks, so does Easter Day for Christians. Since earliest times the period between Easter and Pentecost has been called the "Great Fifty Days."

In earlier liturgical calendars, the Sundays within this season were called Easter Day, First Sunday after Easter, Second Sunday after Easter, and so on. Because this designation obscures the unity of the Great Fifty Days, the Lord's Days are more properly called Easter Day (First Sunday of Easter), followed by Second Sunday of Easter, Third Sunday of Easter, and so forth.

In the lectionary system, specific themes are designated for the Sundays of Easter (for Ascension Day), as follows: Year B begins with the report of the meal at Emmaus and continues into Jesus' appearance in the upper room, where he eats fish (Luke 24:35-38). In Year C we read of Jesus' appearance at seaside, when Jesus prepared breakfast for the disciples (John 21:1-19).

Therefore this Sunday is an excellent time to observe the Lord's Supper, and both in the manner of its celebration and in the sermon to highlight the Eucharist (Holy Communion) as a means by which we know the Risen Lord, rather than as a sentimental memorial to the suffering Jesus as he faces Calvary.

Suitable congregational songs for the day include:

40—"I Do, Don't You?" (especially stanza 2)

59—"Lift Him Up" (especially stanza 2)

88—"Let Us Break Bread Together"

128—"You Hear the Lambs a-Cryin'" (related to the final portion of the Gospel reading in Year C)

133—"The Time for Praying" (Gospel, Year C, as above)

245—"Hungry and Thirsty, Lord, We Come"

Fourth Sunday of Easter ("Good Shepherd Sunday")

In each year, the Risen Lord as shepherd of the flock is set forth in a passage from John 10 as well as in Psalm 23. The resurrection, properly interpreted, is a great mystery beyond human comprehension. But the One whose risen nature we cannot fathom, before whom we stand in absolute awe, is yet to us like a trusted shepherd who calls us by name and cares for us daily. Thus the necessary tension between the cosmic and the personal dimensions of the gospel is maintained. Suitable to this day are "All Is Well" (#5) and verse 1 of "Rise an' Shine" (#79).

Fifth Sunday of Easter

In Years A and B, the Gospel sets forth one of the great "I AM" passages of John's Gospel: "I AM the way, the truth, and the life." "I AM the true vine." The fact that the Risen One has opened to us a new age does not negate our Hebraic heritage. John's use of "I AM" is deliberately reminiscent of Exodus 3:14. In Year C, Jesus gives us the command to love one another. Christ, by fulfilling all things, empowers us for our ministry in the world. Particularly in Year C, "A Prayer for Love" (#70) is appropriate.

Sixth Sunday of Easter

As on the Fifth Sunday, the implications of the Lord's Resurrection for our life of faith and ministry are set forth from a Johannine perspective. "A Prayer for Love" is especially suitable in Year B.

Ascension Day (Because this occasion falls on Thursday, in many churches it is transferred to the Seventh Sunday of Easter.)

The work of salvation in Christ is now fulfilled; Jesus, who on earth was available to only a few people for a few years within a few square miles of his home, now by the power of the Holy Spirit, is accessible to all people, at all times, and in all places. The Resurrection means that the Risen and Glorified One is set free from earthly constraint.

Seventh Sunday of Easter (if not reserved for Ascension)

The Gospel reading in all years is from John 17, the "high priestly prayer" of Jesus on behalf of his disciples and the church they are to form. Because the unity of the church is stressed on this day, "One God, One Faith, One Baptism" (#220) may be used as a choral response.

Pentecost

This closes the season of Easter and recapitulates a consistent Easter theme: that the church exists because of the resurrection, and that the hearing of the gospel unites into one people those who receive its word. These themes are made evident in the account of the empowerment of the apostles by the Holy Spirit and the understanding of their message by people of many tongues.

Pentecost is an excellent occasion for Holy Communion; it is also a Sunday for baptisms and confirmations, if these have not occurred at Easter Day.

Songs suitable to the day include:

6—"Easter People, Raise Your Voices" (as an indication that this day closes the Easter season)

26—"Jesus Loves the Little Children" (sung by children)

65—"In Christ There Is No East or West"

81—"I'm Gonna Sing"

121—"Ev'ry Time I Feel the Spirit"

123—"Balm in Gilead"

185—"Move Me"

226—"Spirit of the Living God"

Lent

A season as important as the Great Fifty Days requires spiritual preparation. Intended exactly for that purpose, Lent is a period of forty weekdays, plus six Sundays. The theme of the final week—Holy Week—is the passion and sacrifice of our Lord; but, contrary to previous practice, that is not the theme of the entire season.

Lent begins on Ash Wednesday, which announces to us the fact of sin and death, but under the gracious redemption of God. Throughout the season we contemplate the ramifications of this—our sinfulness and the inevitability of physical death; our renunciation of sin and death to sin through the baptismal covenant; and finally the way in which our Lord's death takes up our death, transforms us, and offers us new life through the Resurrection.

Lent in its origins was primarily a time for final preparation by those to be baptized at Easter. The season should be devoted primarily to that, where there are candidates for baptism. Even without such, Lent is a time of aspiration and deepening devotion among those already baptized, as they recall their own promises to God. During Lent the invitation to repentance and salvation is extended to sinners, and the people of God give testimony of grace before all who stand in need. Thus Lent is a season of spiritual call and response.

On the Sundays of Lent, readings echo the themes of cleansing, transformation, discipline, covenant, and commitment. "Pilgrimage" is an important theme, tied to Israel's release and sojourn on the way to the promised land. Appropriate hymns include:

3—"We're Marching to Zion"

18—"Lord, I'm Coming Home"

31—"He Looked Beyond My Fault"

35—"I Shall Not Be Moved"

39—"Higher Ground"

54—"On Jordan's Stormy Banks"

58—"The Storm is Passing Over"

61—"Come to Jesus"

64—"Thy Way, O Lord"

66—"More About Jesus"

76—"Lord, I Want to Be a Christian"

95—"I Want Jesus to Walk with Me"

110—"Standin' in the Need of Prayer"

111—"Trampin' "

123—"Balm in Gilead"

130—"Tryin' to Get Home"

134—"Steal Away"

135—"City Called Heaven"

136—"Come Out de Wilderness" (Stanza I can be sung by members who address their question to the baptized. Then stanzas 2 and 3 are sung by or on behalf of the congregation, with all singing the responses throughout.)

143—"I've Been 'Buked"

154—"Somebody's Knocking at Your Door"

157—"On Ma Journey"

170—"Nobody Knows the Trouble I See"

171—"Nobody Knows the Trouble I See, Lord!"

177—"Until I Found the Lord"
182—"Give Me a Clean Heart"
185—"Move Me"
186—"If You Ask Him"
192—"We've Come This Far By Faith"
193—"Surely God Is Able"
205—"We Are Climbing Jacob's Ladder"
208—"Just As I Am"
225—"O Lord, Have Mercy"

Holy Week

The final week of Lent is of a special character. Now we gather at the foot of the cross—even on the opening Sunday of Holy Week. Previously this was called "Palm Sunday" and tended to focus entirely on Jesus' entry into Jerusalem. But that entry is "triumphal" only in a very ironic sense, and to celebrate the day with nothing but festivity is to misunderstand the Gospel accounts of the entry. Jesus goes into the city in order to die. Therefore, on this day his death is proclaimed in the congregation (particularly since many who attend will not return for services on Holy Thursday or Good Friday). As a signal of a fuller meaning than the occasion once had, the day is now called Palm-Passion Sunday or Passion-Palm Sunday.

The rest of the week continues the theme of Jesus' sacrificial death. On Thursday evening we give thanks for the gift of the Lord's Supper which, though instituted in the upper room, proclaims not only his suffering but also his Resurrection; for the meal in the upper room is transformed by the meal at Emmaus. Therefore, the Thursday evening service may be somewhat more joyful than often has been the case. On Good Friday we commemorate the crucifixion by entering into the ministry of intercessory prayer that Jesus engaged in upon the cross. Music especially pertinent to Holy Week includes:

19—"Jesus, Keep Me Near the Cross"
43—"I Believe It"

77—"Ride On, King Jesus" (Palm-Passion Sunday)
87—"Calvary"
88—"Let Us Break Bread Together" (Holy Thursday)
101—"He Nevuh Said a Mumbaling' Word"
126—"Were You There?"
153—"Oh, Mary, Don't You Weep, Don't You Mourn"
215—"My Faith Looks Up to Thee"

Sundays and Other Occasions Surrounding Christmas Day

Christmas

Christmas is a season of twelve days, beginning on December 25. It is followed by Epiphany on January 6, and the Sunday of the Baptism of the Lord on the Sunday following January 6. (Epiphany frequently is celebrated on a Sunday, though it usually falls on a weekday.) When January 6 occurs on Sunday, that day may serve for a combined celebration of the Lord's Epiphany and Baptism, or the two events may be observed on succeeding Sundays.

The nature and redeeming work of Jesus Christ are the foci of Christmas and the following days. The festivals are not primarily days about his humble birth, important as that is, but about *who* has been born. Jesus Christ is the Savior of both Jews (symbolized by the shepherds, and by Simeon and Anna in the temple) and the Gentiles (symbolized by the Magi); he is monarch, deity, and the suffering servant who offers up his life (symbolized by the gifts of gold, frankincense, and myrrh); and he is the Beloved Son of God who inaugurates a new creation, as declared at this baptism. This triple identification is set forth on Christmas Day, Epiphany, and the Sunday of the Baptism, respectively. Songs for Christmas and the days following are "Glory Be to Our God on High" (#2) and "Go, Tell It on the Mountain" (#75).

Advent

As the Great Fifty Days of Easter are preceded by a time of preparation, so also is the season of Christmas. But Advent is briefer, beginning always on the fourth Sunday before December 25 and including between 22 and 28 days; further, Lent is a heavily penitential season but Advent is not regarded as such.

Advent is not Christmas-come-early. Its name means "coming," and the season sets forth a parallel between the fulfilled coming of the Messiah at Bethlehem and the anticipated coming of the Lord at the end of time. Thus it has themes drawn from the prophets and John the Baptist, on the one hand, and from the church's hope for the return of the Lord in judgment and victory, on the other hand.

When the season is observed correctly, the gospel's emphasis on social justice and the triumph of God's righteousness over all evil and oppression is sounded with particular insistence; but when Advent is misunderstood as a premature Christmas celebration the crucial themes are often muted or silenced entirely. The readings in the lectionary clearly set forth the character of Advent; and music appropriate to the central themes is plentiful:

10—"Some Day" (also 207)
20—"It is Well with My Soul" (stanza 4)
24—"Battle Hymn of the Republic" (also 213) (stanzas 1 and 3)
28—"Farther Along" (stanza 4)
29—"I Know Who Holds Tomorrow"
60—"I Have Found at Last the Savior" (stanza 5)
79—"Rise an' Shine"
103—"Rockin' Jerusalem"
145—"My Lord! What a Mourning"
156—"There's a Great Camp Meeting"
169—"Oh! What a Beautiful City"
198—"Soon and Very Soon"

VIII

The Spirituals in Songs of Zion

74 MY SOUL'S BEEN ANCHORED IN DE LORD

A song of pure joy, "My Soul's Been Anchored in de Lord" reveals the determination and commitment the slaves had toward their newfound faith. This lively song would be well placed in a revival or in any service focusing especially on Christian discipleship. In more evangelical congregations, it might even be used in a funeral service as a song of victory.

75 GO, TELL IT ON THE MOUNTAIN

This is one of the few spirituals dealing with the birth of Christ. The slave-composers of the spirituals were either put off by the sacrilegious nature of Christmas celebrations in the South, or were deliberately under-informed of the meaning of the birth of Christ by whites who feared its social implications of the poor, lowly slaves. Sung with enthusiasm and excitement appropriate for the season, this is an ideal Christmas song.

76 LORD, I WANT TO BE A CHRISTIAN

As the slaves understanding of Christ developed, so did their awareness of the misuse of Christianity by their white masters. These words were a product of the slaves' desire to be true to their faith. It is to be sung prayerfully and fervently. One particularly powerful rendition is to have the music played through without singing after the third verse, and have the singing resume at a slightly faster tempo in the fourth verse and chorus.

77 RIDE ON, KING JESUS

Drawing on biblical imagery from the Old and New Testaments, Ride on, King Jesus refers to Isaiah's often-used image of the highway, and to Jesus' triumphal entry into Jerusalem. This song of commitment and perseverance may be used for Palm/Passion Sunday as a majestic processional or recessional.

78 I COULDN'T HEAR NOBODY PRAY

Here the spiritual begins in sadness and ends in joy. Slave communities and families were often cruelly and systematically split, leaving individuals with an overwhelming sense of social and spiritual loneliness. The song speaks in the individual's feeling of having to stand alone in the faith, a faith that sometimes appeared to be abandoned by others caught in the throes of trouble. This song is particularly appropriate when there is a break in community such as caused by death, moving away, entering the service, etc.; for though these situations are very difficult at first, the empty spaces they leave are certain to be filled "wid ma Jesus."

79 RISE AN' SHINE

This joy song is a direct reference to the 25th chapter of Leviticus, wherein God describes to Moses the "year of jubilee." The Hebrews, after six years of labor, were to rest in the sabbath year. After this cycle had been completed seven times (that is, after forty-nine years) the 50th year was to be the year of jubilee, a year to "proclaim liberty throughout the land." Surely the American Negro slaves anticipated that year of jubilee with as much excitement as did the Hebrews. This song can be used in any service where the theme is liberation or celebration.

80 FREE AT LAST

The broad view of life and liberty that was held by the slaves rings clearly in this song. These verses speak of physical and spiritual freedom. That dual meaning is apparent in the obvious other-worldly emphasis of the first verse and the coded usage of the Jordan motif in the second verse. The image of the Jordan River was often used to allude to a means of escape to the North. The dual nature of this spiritual renders it appropriate for occasions focusing on liberation in its more political sense (such as Black History Month, Martin Luther King, Jr. birthday observances, etc.) or in its more spiritual sense (such as death).

81 I'M GONNA SING

One of the most commonplace sermons a slave heard was based on the Pauline injunction "Servant, obey your masters"; but the slaves also knew that the Bible called Christians to "please God rather than men." Thus, when out of fear and misunderstanding, many of the religious expressions of the Negro were either frowned upon or blatantly forbidden by whites, the slaves chose rather to "obey the Spirit of the Lord." As this song includes several components of the total worship experience, it is appropriate at almost any occasion when the faithful gather to worship "in Spirit and in truth."

82   I'VE GOT A ROBE

"I've Got a Robe" reveals the slave's understanding of heaven as a place prepared for *them*—individually and collectively. In this song, their biblical imaginations ran free! They had personal possessions in heaven. They would be made to feel at home in heaven. Unlike their restricted movements on the southern plantations, they would be able to walk, play, and shout "all over God's heaven." This lively song is ideal when rejoicing for the life of a saint who has gone to be with God.

83   SOMETIMES I FEEL LIKE A MOTHERLESS CHILE

One of the most familiar of all spirituals, this song is pure sorrow. The images are striking in their simplicity: "motherless" "almos' gone" "long ways from home." This song is effective in almost any somber setting.

84   EZEK'EL SAW DE WHEEL

Using the imagery of Ezekiel's visions (chapters 1 and 10), the slaves found a word of prophecy in their own day. This song, with its almost humorous verses, is probably best used as special music in a regular worship service or in a concert.

85   HE'S GOT THE WHOLE WORLD IN HIS HANDS

A song of praise for the God of creation. The slave had reason to be glad to know that God was still in control and all things were in God's hands. It is still a very popular song for children's choirs, and is very effective with dramatic hand and arm motions used in unison.

86 HOLD ON

Full of biblical imagery, this Negro spiritual was one
of hope and encouragement with a word of warning.
We can only imagine how much meaning this song
must have held for the slaves as these words rose up
out of the fields of the South. How tempted they must
have been to let go the dirt plow *and* the gospel plow as
they bore their burdens in the heat of the day. This
song is useful in conjunction with any major
undertaking of the household of faith such as church
building, discipleship programs, etc. It can also be
used in any event of celebration in recognition of
outstanding service.

87 CALVARY

The Crucifixion and the Resurrection were for the
slaves the core of the Christian faith. The passion
narrative of the gospels is literally retold in lyrics.
Sung slowly and fervently, this selection is ideal for
any Holy Week service and particularly Good Friday.

88 LET US BREAK BREAD TOGETHER

This song has become a standard in the black church's
celebration of Holy Communion. Its simple lyrics and
unencumbered melody provide an ideal background
for receiving the Body and Blood of Christ. It can be
sung as a solo or by a choir, but it is best rendered with
full congregational participation befitting the mood
and meaning of the Communion service.

89 OLE-TIME RELIGION

Later generations of Christian slaves could see
younger slaves less inclined to strictly adhere to the
principles of Christian faith. They feared that this
could lead to wandering from the fold. This popular

93

song was a call back to the simple faith the slaves embraced when they first heard about Jesus. This song's "sing ability" renders it appropriate for most any occasion and has become a favorite in the black church for homecomings, camp meetings, etc.

90 HIS NAME SO SWEET

This song's lively and joyful refrain is the slaves' response to their personal encounter with God. The verses suggest this to be a later spiritual, influenced by the Baptist and the Methodist ("Class leader/'Sidin' elder, do you love Jesus?"). One possible application of this song is that it be used as a parting selection to end a service on a joyful note.

91 THERE'S A MEETING HERE TONIGHT

The double entendre for which so many of slave songs are famous is obvious in this piece. The slaves intended to have the whites who might have heard these words believe that they were merely planning a harmless worship, when in reality this was a call to worship *and* to discuss their enslavement and plan escapes.

92 FREEDOM TRAIN A-COMIN'

Here is a freedom song in its purest, most undisguised form. As it became apparent that slave-holding days were numbered, the Negroes became more open and bold in their pronouncements. This song was a call to preparation for emancipation. It does not belong in the category of "religious" spirituals; it is purely political in its scope; but the very subject of freedom was such a temporal and religious matter that these songs were in fact spirituals (as opposed to belonging in the category of Negro folk songs).

93 KEEP A-INCHIN' ALONG

As much as the slaves desired a better life on earth, they looked toward a new life in heaven with the Lord. With this song of determination, the slaves saw the struggle for salvation to be as serious and involved a process as their struggle for liberation. Both involved "trials and troubles on the way," but they had confidence that "like a poor inch-worm" they would reach their goals.

94 LITTLE DAVID, PLAY ON YOUR HARP

Old Testament characters and stories of valor and adventure were favorite subjects of the Negro spirituals. The slaves obviously loved to retell these stories in song. This particular spiritual is the product of much later editing, for the last verse was composed by a student at Fisk University, although the chorus is original.

95 I WANT JESUS TO WALK WITH ME

The slaves viewed themselves as a pilgrim people on their way out of bondage and into the promised land. They understood Jesus to be their burden bearer, the only one who could help them reach their destination. They implored this assistance in this spiritual: "I want Jesus to walk with me." This song is not so much a request as it is an affirmation that the Jesus of their salvation would be with them. They could look "back to the historical-divine experiences and the reports of their predecessors" and assert "He walked with my mother, he'll walk with me" (this verse, though not included in the printed text of this song in *Songs of Zion*, is as familiar in the black church as the three that are printed.) This song is very popular in the black church during prayer services and devotional services preceding the regular and worship services.

96 JOSHUA FIT DE BATTLE OF JERICHO

Again, the adventures of Old Testament characters provide the material for the slave's songs. The masses of Negro slaves having no more than minimal literacy skills at best often learned and taught the content of the scriptures through these songs. They found in the Bible stories proof that theirs was a mighty God who assured them "de battle am in my hand." This ever-popular spiritual is appropriate for most any occasion.

97 PETER, GO RING THEM BELLS

This joy song expresses the slaves' unbridled emotions relative to their religious experience. As J. W. Work notes, in these songs little attention was given to the everyday life which had so few attractions. The slaves were able to look beyond their dismal situation and dwell on the joy they felt in their souls. As with most of the joy songs, "Peter, Go Ring Them Bells" is very well placed as a parting selection or as a response to the sermon.

98 GLORY, GLORY HALLELUJAH

As the Negro slaves became "converted" they were made to realize that the burden of sin was as grievous to be borne as was the burden of enslavement. This conversion experience prompted the slave community to sing, shout, and dance "Glory, Glory Hallelujah! Since I laid my burden down." This song continues to be a favorite in the black church during testimony services, revivals, and in regular Sunday worship as individuals respond to the invitation to Christian discipleship.

99 PLENTY GOOD ROOM

Drawing on Jesus' promise in John 14:2 of a house with many mansions, the slaves realized early that this prepared place was for a prepared people. Thus, this song shows the importance of strict moral goodness for the slaves. "Sinners," "liars," and "cheaters" would have no place in God's kingdom. This well-known spiritual is particularly appropriate as an invitational selection.

100 HUSH, HUSH, SOMEBODY'S CALLIN' MAH NAME

This rhythmic, easy-to-rock-to song is perhaps one of the most popular in the black church. J. Jefferson Cleveland notes the superb "word painting" and amazing imagery of this spiritual. "Hush" is often placed in the devotional service held prior to the ordered worship service. Here it sets a relaxed, yet reverent mood from which the order of worship might proceed. This song might also be used as a gathering for a funeral service.

101 HE NEVUH SAID A MUMBALIN' WORD

Here again, the Crucifixion motif dominates the imagination of the slave. James Cone notes that the slaves were "impressed by the Passion because they too had been rejected, beaten, and shot without a chance to say a word in defense of their humanity." The message and the slow, haunting, and reverent tone of this song make it ideal for the most somber of days in the Christian year, Good Friday.

102 OH, FREEDOM

Slaves realized that the slightest suggestion of political freedom in the presence of white people could cost them their lives. However, this song's thinly veneered message of emancipation reveals that the slaves were less concerned over physical punishment than might be expected. Freedom songs like this one were the Negroes' response to the Civil War and emancipation.

This song has remained popular among black people and was certainly a favorite during the Civil Rights Movement. Inasmuch as the black church continues to recognize political and spiritual freedom as its main objective, this song is appropriate for most any service, but particularly services with a thematic emphasis on peoples' struggles for liberation.

103 ROCKIN' JERUSALEM

Quite similar in mood and content to "Peter, Go Ring Them Bells," "Rockin' Jerusalem" stands as a song of pure, simple joy. The cause for rejoicing in this song is the growth of the "invisible institution," the church. Alluding to Jesus' observation in Luke 15:7, that "joy shall be in heaven over one sinner that repenteth, more than over ninety and nine just persons, which need no repentance," as their friends and loved ones came into "the fold" the slaves revelled in the prospect of the "Church getting higher!" This song also is most appropriate at the reception of new members in the church. Since Mary and Martha are the bell ringers in this song, it should not be overlooked in women's day and sisterhood services.

104 SWING LOW, SWEET CHARIOT

This sorrow song with a note of joy is based on the experience of Elijah in II Kings 2:1-11. J. W. Work tells the story of this song's origin: a slave mother had been sold and was to be separated from her baby daughter and taken "down South." Choosing rather to die and to take her child's life, rather than to be eternally separated, the young mother went to throw herself over into the Cumberland River. An old "mammy" knowing the woman's intentions stopped her with the words, "Don't you do it, honey; wait, let de chariot of de Lord swing low." This song grew as it passed from mouth to mouth until it reached its present state. "Swing Low, Sweet Chariot" remains a standard among many black congregations in the funeral service.

105 MAH GOD IS SO HIGH

The slaves took their religion seriously. When they embraced the Christian faith, they did so with incomparable zeal. For many of them, life held no other viable option but to serve the Lord. They understood fully what Jesus meant when in John 14:6 he said, "I am the way, the truth, and the life: no man cometh unto the Father, but by me." "Mah God Is So High" is a song of praise, adoration, and devotion. It can be used in any service as an anthem, and in special situations dealing with discipleship and commitment.

106 DIDN'T MY LORD DELIVER DANIEL?

Despite the often apparent hopelessness of the slaves' situation, they were consistent in their belief that God desired freedom for them; and that through all their trials, God was with them. This perspective on liberation was reinforced time and time again in the Bible. In this spiritual, the slaves' case for God's concern for their plight was plainly put: if God could, and indeed did, deliver Daniel (and Jonah, and the Hebrew children), then why not every man? This song is most often rendered now in concert or choral form and makes for good special music at almost any service.

107 HARD TRIALS

The scriptural references in the spirituals are not always contextually accurate. The spirituals make no claim of exegetical skillfulness. "Hard Trials" is one example of the slaves' unique way of using biblical passages in their songs (see Matthew 8:20 and Luke 9:58). The last two verses of this song are obviously later additions coming with the influences of denominationalism and institutionalized religion among blacks. Nevertheless, the meaning of the song is clear, and its point is well taken: life without Christ is a life of "hard trials."

108 LIVE A-HUMBLE

J. W. Work classifies this as both a sorrow song and a song of humility, most likely due to its obvious connection with the sacrifice of Jesus. The thought that King Jesus would come to die, was enough to humble any slave. The joyful melody of "Live a-Humble" mitigates the melancholy influence of its words, making it appropriate for either festive or somber occasions.

109 JUBILEE

Because of the overwhelming importance of religion in the Negroes' lives, the "invisible institution" of slave days soon after became the visible church. An interesting and unique aspect of slave religion was what simply came to be called, "the shout." Joseph Washington quotes from Robert E. Parks' book, *Race and Culture*, to describe "the shout."

> But the benches are pushed back to the wall when the formal meeting is over, and old and young, men and women, sprucely dressed young men, grotesquely half-clad field hands, the women generally with gay handkerchiefs twisted about their heads and with short skirts, boys with tattered shirts and men's trousers, young girls bare-footed, all stand up in the middle of the floor, and when the "sperichil" is struck up, begin first walking and by and by shuf-

100

fling around, one after the other, in a ring. The foot is hardly taken from the floor and the progression is mainly due to a jerking, hitching motion which agitates the entire shouter and soon brings out streams of perspiration. Sometimes they dance silently, sometimes as they shuffle they sing the chorus of the spiritual, and sometimes the song itself is also sung by the dancers. But more frequently a band, composed of some of the best singers and of tired shouters, stands at the side of the room to "base" the others, singing the body of the song, and dropping their hands together or on their knees. Song and dance are alike extremely energetic and often, when the shout lasts into the middle of the night, the monotonous thud, thud, of the feet prevents sleep within a half a mile of the praise-house.[1]

As the black church became more structured and sophisticated in its worship life expressions such as, the shout, the mourners' bench, and the amen corner, began to become passé. "Jubilee" was a call back to old time religion. The almost humorous verses and the marching tempo of the song make this a good concert song.

110 STANDIN' IN THE NEED OF PRAYER

One of *the* most widely known Negro spirituals, this one is essentially individualistic, which by and large was rarely critical of others. The slaves saw the assurance of salvation as largely a personal responsibility. Realizing imperfection, the people affirmed in this song a total and complete reliance upon the grace of God. "Standin' in the Need of Prayer" is an obvious choice for an altar call song in most any church service.

111 TRAMPIN'

"Trampin' " is another song expressing the slaves' dedication and commitment to completing their

Christian journey. Implicit in the words of this song is the slaves' struggle to stay on the "straight and narrow path," even in the face of obstacles and difficulties. Though the slaves expected to have a better life on earth someday, nothing the world offered could compare with the beauty and joy of heaven. The concept of reaching God, and the firm beat of this song, suggests its use as a processional or recessional.

112 GO DOWN, MOSES

This popular spiritual chronicles the events of the Exodus and preaches freedom "in a biblical way." The song supposedly originated as a result of a Negro preacher "interpreting slavery in terms of Egyptian bondage, every now and then throwing out the hint that freedom was coming to the Negro, too."

The question of the origin of the melody of this song uncovers an interesting possibility. This was revealed to J. W. Work by a social worker in the following way:

> I was holding a woman's meeting one evening, and to help things move along, asked the women to sing one of their own songs. To my surprise, one began the tune of 'Go Down, Moses,' and the others followed. I was greatly interested, and asked them what the song was. I was told that it was one of their folk songs, 'Cain and Abel.' Desiring to satisfy myself in this matter, I held another meeting of Hebrew women who were not at the former meeting, and as a part of their exercises I sang, 'Go Down, Moses.' They recognized it as their song, 'Cain and Abel.' Whether of Hebrew or of Negro origin, there seems to be no way of determining, but it bears all the evidences of the Negro music. In plaintiveness, in intervallic changes, in melody, in scale, in rhythm, and in spirit, it has all evidences of Negro origin.[2]

"Go Down, Moses" remains a standard in the black church as people today continue to suffer under the bondage of the modern-day Pharaohs of racism, sexism, classism, and poverty.

113 DE OL' ARK'S A-MOVERIN'

"De Ol' Ark's a-Moverin' " is another spiritual with an original refrain based on a biblical passage; the remaining stanzas are the result of later editing. This particular song was a caution against worldliness and impropriety. Just as in the days of Noah, there were those who chose not to heed the words of warning, so were some of the people in earlier days. Although the days of such strict observance of dress codes are long gone, the black church still expects a modicum of modesty in outward appearance. Nevertheless, "De Ol' Ark's a-Moverin' " is probably best reserved for concert or special music use.

114 AIN-A DAT GOOD NEWS?

With so few possessions to call their own, and scant prospects of wealth in any degree, the biblical promise of a crown, etc. in the kingdom made an intolerable situation more tolerable. This song is unrestrained joy! Going home to be with Jesus had no downside: It was all good news. Its spirited tempo and easy-to-follow melody make "Ain't Dat Good News?" suitable for an anthem, special choral selection, or concert rendition.

115 DEEP RIVER

The Jordan River motif is employed with profound depth and impact in this song. The strikingly simple lyrics and slow, almost labored melody bring to life the deep yearning of the slaves to reach that physical *and* spiritual "promis'd land where all is peace." Although possibilities for using "Deep River" are many, the black church seems most satisfied with it as a funeral dirge.

116 DE GOSPEL TRAIN

The slaves viewed the kingdom of God as a future event *and* as a present reality. They saw themselves as "bound for the kingdom that was breaking into the already new present, and they affirmed their willingness to 'git on board' that 'gospel train.'" Having nothing to lose and everything to gain, the slaves accepted the risk because the gospel train meant the possibility of freedom. With the possibility of freedom still ever before us, "De Gospel Train" is another spiritual that commends itself for use in most any church service.

117 ROLL, JORDAN, ROLL

Here again, the theme of death as an escape from this life is repeated. Washington suggests that this theme gives "clear evidence" that the missionaries taught primarily a religion about another time and place. "Roll, Jordan, Roll" is a song of hope and faith that death would carry the individual to a brighter and more beautiful day.

118 CHANGED MAH NAME

The Africans transported to America were systematically stripped of every vestige of their cultural past. They were forced to speak an alien language, be subject to gross brutalities, observe foreign customs, and the highest insult of all—to be called by a strange name. The only way to reconcile themselves with their new identities was to accept these "Christian names" as the will of God. As they began to give these names to their own children, they were sad that they were in effect abandoning their African heritage; but they were comforted by the knowledge that in Jesus they had found one who would be for them a Savior. The ritual of naming still remains an important one in many black communities. Therefore, "Changed Mah Name" could easily be used in a baptismal service.

119 DO, LORD, REMEMBER ME

Quoting the words of the thief on the cross, recorded in Luke 23:42, the slaves realized that even in the face of death, the last word belongs to God. They understood that God was always with them and they believed that they had "encountered the infinite significance of his liberation." As oppressed people today continue to feel despised and rejected by the individuals, systems, and structures of this world, the cry remains, "Lord, remember me." This song is especially useful in memorial services and funerals.

120 CLIMBIN' UP D' MOUNTAIN

Using Old Testament imagery this song graphically describes the struggle for deliverance. The slaves believed that although the road was rough, the same God who delivered Daniel, Shadrach, Meshach, and Abednego would in time deliver them. They saw themselves as a pilgrim people on a journey that began in the fields and kitchens of Southern plantations, and would end at the foot of the judgment seat of God. "Climbin' Up d' Mountain" is an excellent processional or recessional for the regular worship service.

121 EV'RY TIME I FEEL THE SPIRIT

This widely known spiritual describes "the power and energy released in black devotion to the God of emotion." Black people have never had any concept of a God who could not be *felt*. It is this *feeling* of the spirit of God that renders the black religious experience incomparable to any other. Given the spontaneity characteristic of worship in the traditional black church, "Ev'ry Time I Feel the Spirit" is appropriate at most any time at most any service.

122 FIX ME, JESUS

Black folks have always had a sense of being chosen people of God; and have always been confident that they would, individually and collectively, spend eternity in heaven. This confidence, however, in no way minimized the necessity to live so that each would be prepared for their final end. "Fix Me, Jesus" expresses the earnest desire of the slaves to be fit for their ultimate destination. The somber, reverent, almost pleading melody has made it a favorite for devotional services, testimony service, altar calls, and invitational selections. Verolga Nix's arrangement is well rendered as a concert piece.

123 BALM IN GILEAD

This popular spiritual answers the question posed in Jeremiah 8:22, "Is there no balm in Gilead; is there no physician there?" It is a song of hope and encouragement; for as Cone notes, "hope, in the black spirituals, is not a denial of history. Black hope accepts history, but believes that the historical is in motion, moving toward a divine fulfillment." "Balm in Gilead" is an excellent revival song.

124 GOOD NEWS

Slaves believed that the chariot of the Lord that swung low to get Elijah was still making its rounds; and that was good news. They believed that upon their arrival on the golden streets, they would be outfitted in robes, wings, crowns, etc. "Good News" is a lively and joyful song and its popular usage as a choral selection makes it good special music in the worship service.

125 YOU'D BETTER MIN'

Black people have always known God to be a God of judgment. They feared God's wrath and retribution, knowing that they would have to answer for the "things done in the body." "You'd Better Min' " is a word of caution to the faithful community, a reminder that God cannot be deceived, and that God judges intentions as well as actions. This song reminds the modern day church of its responsibility to be a prophetic voice in the world. Although the strict moralism of the slaves has all but disappeared in our time, "You'd Better Min' " is still useful as a call to personal goodness in our congregation.

126 WERE YOU THERE?

Although their knowledge of scriptures was rudimentary, the slaves did not see biblical events as unrelated to themselves. These were their stories. The Bible spoke of their joys and their sorrows, their triumphs and their trials. They were able to see in their own situation the significance of the Crucifixion. So real for them was the shame and suffering of Jesus that they more than figuratively asked, "Were you there when they crucified my Lord?" This song of sheer, undisguised sorrow is perhaps the most widely used in the black church's Good Friday service. As it appears in *Songs of Zion*, "Were You There?" ends at the tomb which is appropriate for Good Friday. It lends itself to Easter usage, however, with the addition of a sixth verse sung more joyously and unrestrained: "Were you there when He rose up from the dead? Were you there when He rose up from the dead? Oh! Sometimes I feel like shouting glory, glory, glory. Were you there when He rose up from the dead?"

127 WE SHALL OVERCOME

It is not known exactly how many or which of the verses of this song originated with the slaves. Contemporary usage has undoubtedly left its mark. What is unquestionably clear, however, is that from its beginnings "We Shall Overcome" has been a song of faith, courage, and determination. This song is as much a socio-political statement as it is a religious one, having its place as the theme song of the Civil Rights Movement. Black radicals, white liberals, the churched and the unchurched all stand on common ground when they sing "We Shall Overcome." With this recent historical background, it remains a favorite for any event when peoples of diverse backgrounds come together for a common cause.

128 YOU HEAR THE LAMBS A-CRYIN'

The slave saw caring for another as mandate from Christ. They realized that their common plight demanded that they each look to the other's needs. Interestingly, this directive to serve came to slaves not as the course commands of their masters and overseers, but as the plaintive plea of the eternal lamb of God. "You Hear the Lambs a-Cryin' " is useful for any occasion promoting mission and outreach.

129 WADE IN THE WATER

This song draws on imagery from both the Old and the New Testament. The chorus is taken from the story in the fifth chapter of John of the impotent man being cured by the famous pool of Bethesda (to which an angel would come at certain times to "trouble the water"). The verses refer directly to the exodus of God's people from Egypt. In either case, the symbol of water was associated with salvation and deliverance. It comes as no surprise then that "Wade in the Water" has been and remains a favorite in the black church for services of baptism (particularly in those congregations that practice baptism by immersion).

130 TRYIN' TO GET HOME

Many of the slave songs centered on the simple reality that life was hard. They had little time for matters of social status, the accumulation of wealth and power, etc. Their days were occupied with the most basic of quests—survival. It would be unfair, however, to characterize the slaves' will to live as a purely existential matter. They did not live simply for the sake of living. They saw themselves as sojourners, traversing the wilderness of life, "Tryin' to Get Home." This song plainly describes the struggle inherent in the Christians' basic desire to reach that state of oneness with God, that place our souls call "home," making this spiritual appropriate for any service.

131 'TIS THE OLD SHIP OF ZION

The slaves used code names for their means of escape to freedom in the North, the ship of Zion being one of many. As word spread throughout the plantation that means of escape had become available, the brave of heart were summoned by the refrain: "Git on board, git on board." The coded message of this song has somehow faded into non-use and the other worldly message has been emphasized, making "Old Ship of Zion" a common funeral selection.

132 THIS LITTLE LIGHT OF MINE

Even though their lives seemed to be surrounded by shadows and darkness, their faith assured them that they were "the light of the world," the "city set on a hill." They saw it as their God-given responsibility to be an example to the world around them. They knew that despite their dismal situation they were bearers of tidings too glad to not be true. As the black church gathers each week to renew its covenant with God to hold out to the end, it promises to be a faithful witness in the world. "This Little Light of Mine" is a superb choice for a parting selection for the weekly worship service.

133 THE TIME FOR PRAYING

Much like the early church, the slaves anticipated the imminent return of Christ which would mean the end of the present age, thus they thought it wise to make the best use of their time. They prepared themselves spiritually through prayer and songs of devotion, and they were careful not to neglect their social obligation to feed the sheep. "The Time for Praying" is quite effective as an altar call song for the regular Sunday worship.

134 STEAL AWAY

John Wesley Work tells the story of a group of slaves in the early 1900s who were allowed to cross the Red River to worship with the Indians who had a mission there. After learning that the missionary to the Indians was a northerner and fearing that he might give the slaves notions of freedom, the master prohibited his slaves from worshipping anymore with the Indians. The slaves were unmoved by their master's change of mind and determined to do in secret what they were no longer allowed to do openly. They decided that despite their master's refusal, they would continue to "steal away to Jesus." This song, as it appears today, was not produced, however, in a single night. The song grew in stages until it reached its present form. James Cone agrees with Fisher's *Negro Slave Songs in the*

110

United States that the probable composer of "Steal Away" was Nat Turner. Not far from its original usage as a call to secret meeting, "Steal Away" is often used now as a song calling the faithful to devotional worship.

135 CITY CALLED HEAVEN

Heaven in the black spirituals is a far-reaching concept, implying much more than pearly gates, jasper walls, and golden streets. James Cone notes, "the idea of heaven provided ways for black people to affirm their humanity when other people were attempting to define them as non-persons." It enabled blacks to say yes to their right to be free by affirming God's promise to the oppressed of the freedom to be. That was what they meant when they sang about a "City Called Heaven." As the black church continues to affirm God's promise, "City Called Heaven" remains a powerful witness to this affirmation.

136 COME OUT DE WILDERNESS

The wilderness experience has always been a popular motif in black religious thought, often referring to the experience of the Hebrews and of Jesus. In either case, the focus was on *leaving* the wilderness. This song is another example of the dualism in the Negro spiritual. It reflected on the conversion experience as coming out of the wilderness of sin, and to the freedom experience as coming out of the wilderness of bondage. This lively and spirited song is useful with the confirmation and reception of adult members into the church, particularly when the congregation extends to these individuals the "right hand of Christian fellowship."

137 MANY THOUSAND GONE

An ex-slave in B. A. Botkin's *Lay My Burden Down* says, "I 'members 'bout the days slavery, and I don't 'lieve they ever gwine have slaves no more on this earth. I think God done took that burden offer his black children, and I'm aiming to praise Him for it to His face in the days of glory which ain't far off." Freedom for the slaves was much more than an ideal; it was an actual event. It was liberation from every appearance of bondage. "Many Thousand Gone," though properly belonging in the category of sorrow songs, is also a song in celebration of those who have, by whatever means, been set free. Although in the contemporary black experience the symbols of bondage are quite different from those described in these lyrics, it remains a moving and powerful witness to those who for the sake of freedom have gone on.

138 STUDY WAR NO MORE

In direct reference to Isaiah 2:4 and Micah 4:3, the slave looked with joyful anticipation to the day when their struggle for liberation and self-determination would be over. Far from being docile and passive idiots (as they have often been portrayed), the slaves were haters of war and destruction. They desired peace with justice and were willing to pay its price. In an age of accelerated nuclear proliferation and the constant threat of mass destruction, "Study War No More" is an ideal song at any time, for any people who love peace.

139 KUM BA YAH, MY LORD

One of the most distinctive characteristics of worship in the black community has been the overwhelming sense of God's actual presence among the faithful.

Black people have always trusted in Jesus' promise in Matthew 18:20 that, "where two or three are gathered together in my name, there am I in the midst of them." As the slaves met for worship, often under the cover of darkness, first on their agenda was to invoke the presence of the Lord by softly and reverently chanting "Kum Ba Yah" (this being the earlier slaves' rendition of the English words, "Come By Here"). Often favored as a children's song, "Kum Ba Yah" is appropriate for any age level as a prelude to worship.

140 GOD IS A GOD

This is a song in praise of the God of creation. The natural world around them—the earth, the sun, the moon, the stars—caused the slaves to stand in awe at the majesty and power of God. And somehow they were able to see themselves in the unfolding of creation. What a comfort it was for them to know that the God who out of nothing created all that was, was the God who cared for them. "God Is a God" is a fine choice for a choral opening selection or for a congregational hymn of praise.

141 NO HIDIN' PLACE

The slaves knew God to be omniscient. They knew that nothing, great or small, could escape the watchful eye of the Almighty. "Judgment was understood as an inevitable element in God's fulfillment of his promises . . . it was a time of reaping the consequences of ethical actions." "No Hidin' Place" was the prophetic cry of a highly moral and traditional people. In our time, it reminds us that sin and unrighteousness cannot be disguised and must be accounted for at the judgment seat of God.

142 GREAT DAY

So real was the prospect of emancipation during the Civil War that the slaves often spoke of their freedom as if it was already won. "Great Day" is a jubilant and spirited song, in celebration of a priori victory. The soon to be former slaves were always careful to acknowledge that, although their freedom appeared to have been won by courageous and brave-hearted men on great battle fields, they knew that the real victory belonged to God. "Great Day" is a song especially appropriate for congregations involved in major undertakings (such as building, expanding, membership drives, etc.) to encourage them that, with God at the head, they shall be victorious.

143 I'VE BEEN 'BUKED

An air of deep sorrow permeates this song. If the slaves knew *anything*, it was the pain of humiliation and dehumanization. And if there is any expression of this pain, it is in the simple redundance of "I've Been 'Buked." But again, true to form, the spiritual does not end on a note of despair; for in the last stanza, this sorrow is turned into renewed determination as the Negro vows never to lay "'ligion down." The increasing popularity of the most basic and original forms of spirituals has made "I've Been 'Buked" a favorite for concerts, small group selections, and choral renditions in ordered worship.

144 I BEEN IN DE STORM SO LONG

The seemingly capricious and reckless forces of nature often informed the text of the Negro spirituals. Accustomed to seeing storms in the South rise up as if out of nowhere and disappear just as quickly, the slaves felt that their whole life was darkened and dampened by a torrential downpour of trials and tribulations. The mournful strains of "I Been in de Storm So Long" has often been favored as a funeral selection, especially appropriate for the passing of one who has faithfully withstood prolonged illness.

145 MY LORD! WHAT A MOURNING

The wording most often rendered is "what a morning," referring, as so many of the slave songs did, to the "great gettin' up morning," in which Christ would return to the earth. This song, however, attests to "an apocalyptic cosmic expectation which would accompany the ending of this present age just preceding the sound of the first trumpet," (see I Thessalonians 4:16). "My Lord! What a Mourning" suggests itself as an ideal selection for the Advent season in which the church simultaneously looks back to the first, and forward to the second coming of Christ.

146 WOKE UP DIS MORNIN'

Isaiah 26:3a promises "Thou wilt keep him in perfect peace, whose mind is stayed on thee." Although their peace of mind was threatened on every side, somehow the slaves were able to focus their attentions on God. They knew the necessity of being watchful of the wiles of the Tempter, knowing that if given opportunity, Satan would steal their joy and turn their love into hate. Because of the easy-to-follow, call-and-response pattern throughout the song, "Woke Up Dis Mornin' " is well worth trying as an opening selection in which the entire congregation can participate.

147 AMEN

"Amen" is perhaps the most versatile and widely used of all words in the black church. It signifies agreement with what has been said, approval of the performance of a song. It is an affirmation of particularly home-hitting phrases in a prayer, and it is encouragement for the preacher to "preach on." Because of these and other meanings of *amen*, in the black church this song is appropriate as a spontaneous response at most any given time. One should not, however, overlook its usefulness and alternative to the threefold or sevenfold "Amen" in response to the benediction.

148 I FEEL LIKE MY TIME AIN'T LONG

The slaves acknowledged without fear the brevity and transience of earthly existence. So for them to sing "I Feel Like My Time Ain't Long" should not be considered an indication of despair, but a simple affirmation that "man born of a woman is of few days, and full of trouble." This song, then, is useful for meditation, reflection, and in memorial services.

149 I STOOD ON DE RIBBER OB JERDON

Again, the Jordan River as a means of passage to freedom is a dominant theme of the Negro spiritual. Here the main idea is to be ready to make the escape when the opportunity presents itself. The exaggerated broken English in the lyrics suggests this song's usage as special music or a concert selection. (It would be preferable to provide the audience with a printed copy of the lyrics to aid in comprehension of the lyrics.)

150 I'M A-ROLLING

This song is a simple expression of a slave's perception of life on earth. In a very real way, the slaves saw their purpose in life to remain constant in prayer and to serve the Lord. "I'm a-Rolling" remains one of the lesser known spirituals probably because of its portrayal of Negro life as idyllically simplistic.

151 I WANT TO BE READY

The revelation of John on the Isle of Patmos provides the imagery of this spiritual. The Negroes saw themselves as the future inhabitants of the new Jerusalem and looked forward to becoming its citizens. They realized, however, that this city was prepared for a particular group of people, those who had come "out of great tribulation, and have washed their robes, and made them white in the blood of the Lamb" (Revelations 7:14b). This lively and popular song remains a favorite in the black church as a selection for male voices, particularly for Men's Days, Brotherhood Sundays, etc.

152 KING JESUS IS A-LISTENIN'

Another example of a Negro spiritual that has developed into its present form, this lively and rhythmic refrain, which likely is the original portion of the song, appears to have little to do with the verses that follow. Nevertheless, "King Jesus Is a-Listenin'" has remained rather popular as a concert selection, most often by choruses comprised of men's voices.

153 OH, MARY, DON'T YOU WEEP, DON'T YOU MOURN

In singing this song, the slaves looked simultaneously to the cross and to the exodus experience as proof that theirs was a God of triumph in even the most hopeless of situations. This confidence in a victorious outcome appears pleasantly in the cheerful melody and pleasant imagery of the lyrics of this song. "Oh, Mary, Don't You Weep, Don't You Mourn" can be used quite impressively as a Women's Day selection by either a large chorus, a small group, or a small ensemble.

154 SOMEBODY'S KNOCKING AT YOUR DOOR

The slaves understood the words of Christ as being spoken to them, when in Revelations 3:20, he said, "Behold, I stand at the door, and knock: if any man hears my voice, and opens the door, I will come into him." In this spiritual, there is, as Washington notes, a "sense of drama, an appeal to emotion and a highly personal demand, fundamentals of the existential decision embodied in the community of faith." Inasmuch as the black church has never shirked its duty to declare the wages of sin, "Somebody's Knocking at Your Door" lends itself to use in evangelistic services and in regular worship as a call to Christian discipleship.

155 SOMETIMES I FEEL LIKE A MOANIN' DOVE

See 83, "Sometimes I Feel Like a Motherless Chile."

156 THERE'S A GREAT CAMP MEETING

Assured that their "whole life was only another Exodus under God," the slaves looked forward to being reunited with their loved ones who had escaped to freedom in this world and with those who had escaped *from* this world to eternal freedom in heaven. This is a song of joy, comradery, and encouragement, and is quite popular in traditional black congregations as a processional or recessional as well as a selection in services where the theme is Christian unity and in revivals.

157 ON MA JOURNEY

The refrain of this song is another example of scripture used in a decidedly different context in the Negro spiritual. The slaves were obviously referring to Jesus' charge to his disciples, when he sent them out to preach and to heal, saying to them "Take nothing for your journey'' (Luke 9:3). In this context, Jesus meant ''don't take anything with you *on* your journey.'' As it is used here, it means ''don't take anything in *exchange* for your journey.'' Nevertheless, semantics gives way to religion, and ''On Ma Journey'' retains its integrity as a song of perseverance and determination, a good choice for mission and discipleship services.

158 SOON-A WILL BE DONE

''Soon-a Will Be Done'' expresses the concept of death as a natural, pleasant, and positive way out of the slaves' suffering existence on earth. As James Cone notes, ''God is the companion of sufferers, and *trouble* is not the last word on human existence.'' It remains a popular choice for Holy Week services and funerals.

159 SCANDALIZE' MY NAME

Not only did they face the threat of persecution from without, the slaves also had to deal with the very real threat of misunderstanding and abuse within their own ranks. ''Scandalize' My Name'' is a commentary on such a situation. Not particularly *religious* in nature, this song is probably best reserved for occasions of lesser gravity than regular ordered worship.

160 SIT DOWN, SERVANT, SIT DOWN

In the United States, the slaves' whole reason for being was to work. Their value was judged solely on the basis of their productivity in the households and fields of Southern plantations. Very little concern was given to their own comfort or convenience. So how they must have looked forward to the day when they would hear God say, ''Sit down, servant, sit down.'' The occasion of a life well-spent in Christian service provides an excellent opportunity to use this selection.

161 CERTAINLY, LORD

Slaves converted to Christ were neither ashamed nor embarrassed about their new-found faith. They accepted the charge of Psalm 107:2 ''let the redeemed of the Lord say so.'' ''Certainly, Lord'' was their simple way of expressing the sheer joy of their salvation. In the black church this song had traditionally accompanied events implying the conversion experience and remains useful in this context. The occasion of adult baptism and reception into the household of faith are examples of this song's many uses for today.

162 MARY AND MARTHA

The slaves often used biblical characters to refer to members of their own communities and real-life circumstances. ''Mary and Martha'' were chosen to describe those who had already made their way to freedom, thus signalling the possibility of safe passage for the next riders of the underground railroad. Songs of this nature have often in modern usage changed their thrust to indicate those who have gone ''over Jordan'' to heaven as opposed to the free states in the North.

163 MY GOOD LORD'S DONE BEEN HERE

The occasion of worship for the slaves was a time of actual fellowship with God as well as with fellow Christians. The presence of the Lord was experienced and displayed with unrestrained abandon in the Negro community. This song is the slaves' ecstatic summation of that experience. The verses are obviously later additions and particularly the last one is likely to be considered inappropriate for modern usage. The second verse as well is likely to be excluded because of its blatant denominationalism. What we have then are the refrain and the first verse (which is probably the form in which this song originally appeared), and which remain useful as a closing selection for ordered worship at most any time during the Christian year, possibly excepting the more somber Advent and Lenten seasons.

164 BYE AND BYE

One lesson learned by the slaves was the virtue of patience. They did not know how long their troubles would last; but they did know that "Bye and Bye" relief would come. They saw it as their duty to hold out to the end and to encourage others to do likewise. As we live in a world where positive change seems to come all too slowly, "Bye and Bye" can be used to encourage us to remain faithful to the end.

165 GIVE ME JESUS

Although the slaves undoubtedly desired, at some level, just a few of the simple pleasures and material possessions enjoyed by whites in this life, they realized that without Christ all the luxuries the world could offer meant nothing. So precious to them was the prospect—indeed, the reality—of having Jesus that they were willing to forego and forsake all else for this eternal prize. In our day where an individual's worth is all too often measured by material success, "Give Me Jesus" stands as a profound reminder of life's highest ideals. This song can be particularly useful in regular worship as an offertory selection when the connections between material and spiritual values are most easily made.

166 I KNOW THE LORD'S LAID HIS HANDS ON ME

The slaves felt deep within them the impact of a personal experience with God. This song is another of the slaves' testimonies to that experience; it expressed the certainty of their salvation. The personal witness of the faithful remains one of the most powerful tools for the mission of the church today, thus making "I Know the Lord's Laid His Hands on Me" a practical choice for any congregation's program of evangelism.

167 OVER MY HEAD

In the minds and imaginations of the slaves, everything in the created order bore witness to the reality of God. The "music" of the crickets in the still of the night, the "singing" of the birds in the trees, the "trouble" of storms and rain from the skies, and the vivid image of Jesus the soon-coming King—all were regarded as proof-positive of a divine and superior power. These symbols are no less significant for us today, who with all our knowledge and sophistication continue to marvel at the simple glory of the world around us. "Over My Head," loaded with implications of adoration for the God of nature is an ideal opening selection or song of praise at most any gathering of the faithful.

168 HE AROSE

Faith has always informed black Christians that "through Jesus' death, God has conquered death's power over His people . . . The Resurrection is the divine guarantee that black people's lives are in the hands of the Conqueror of Death." "He Arose" might appear simply to be a chronicle of the events surrounding the death and Resurrection of Christ, but its refrain, "And the Lord will bear my spirit home," implies that through the Resurrection of Jesus, God has done something personal for each of us. What God has done is to free us to "do what is necessary to remain obedient to the Father . . . " and to enable us to "bear the trouble and endure the pain of loneliness in oppression.'' ''He Arose'' (or He 'Rose) remains a standard in the black church for Easter Sunday services.

169 OH! WHAT A BEAUTIFUL CITY

Heaven often captured the imaginations of the slaves and it is obvious that the image of the New Jerusalem was particularly attractive to them. This song focuses on John's description of the twelve gates to the city in Revelations 21:12 (one gate for each of the twelve tribes of Israel). The slaves understood this to mean that all people, from all parts of the earth were invited to preside in the city of God. With the church's current focus on ecumenism, this song can be used to give special attention to the idea of true inclusiveness among the people of God.

170 NOBODY KNOWS THE TROUBLE I SEE

The slaves made ''no attempt to evade the reality of suffering.'' They could not hide from themselves the fact that theirs was often a life of despair. Theirs was a pain and sorrow that ran so deep as to etch its images on their very hearts. Nevertheless, through their sorrow they were still ''confident that Jesus (was) with them and (had) not left them completely alone'' thus they could still sing ''Glory, Hallelujah.'' Because this song stresses the personal and private pain felt by the individual, it is especially useful in the church as a song for altar prayer. This song has also been rendered as a very moving choral anthem.

171 NOBODY KNOWS THE TROUBLE I SEE, LORD!

In this rendition, while the emphasis is still on the personal and private, the individual in trouble calls on the community of the faithful to intercede on their behalf, placing this song more appropriately in the church's time of sharing of concerns or in prayer meeting services.

IX

How to Sing the Songs of Zion

The musical components of the black sacred music tradition served as the pattern for the musical content of *Songs of Zion*. Because this content is steeped primarily, though not exclusively, in this tradition, many are wondering how to use this hymnbook.

From its beginning, the central element of black sacred music in the United States has been the art of highly stylized improvisation. Thus, a problem arises when one tries to formulate rules of improvisation because the essence of that art defies such rules. A few suggestions for performance and interpretation of *The Song of Zion* may be helpful.

Hymns

European ''Classical'' Style

European ''classical'' style hymns are appealing and soul-stirring because of the construction of their texts, as well as their music.

''All Is Well'' (#5) by James Hendrix is written in E-flat major in close harmony. Therefore, vocal blend and balance are important. Its simplicity enhances its beauty and makes the song easy for both choir and congregation to sing. Sing this hymn slowly and at a moderately soft volume. A soloist can sing Verse 1, while the choir and/or congregation hum in the background. Everyone can sing the other verses and refrain. To retain the beauty of this hymn, keep instrumental improvisation to a minimum and do not improvise vocally.

"Prayer for Families" (#9) with text by Lois Stanley and music by Morris C. Queen perfectly combines text and music. The text is a moving prayer and the music, with its active individual lines, strengthens the meaning and seriousness of the prayer. Sing this hymn at a moderate, moving pace with much feeling. While excellent for congregational use, the choir alone can effectively sing this hymn. Have the choir and congregation sing verses 1 and 3 with accompaniment and have the choir sing verse 2 *a capella*. Because of the built-in activity of the voice parts, any improvisation is unnecessary.

"The Day Is Past and Gone" (#13) with music by J. Jefferson Cleveland differs from both the traditional metered or "lined out" setting and from the hymns by Thomas A. Dorsey. The latter emphasized death's sadness, while the Cleveland setting suggests happiness in death. In each setting, the music provides the character. The Cleveland setting leaves the traditional text intact, is written in the key of C major and is divided up into four equal phrases of twelve beats each. The choir may lead the congregation by singing this hymn in parts, while the congregation sings the melody in unison. Do not sing this hymn as though it were a funeral dirge, and improvise minimally, if at all.

Traditional Non-Indigenous Hymns Adopted by Blacks

From approximately 1875-1930, about 225 Euro-American hymns were adopted by black Christians for use in their own unique worship services. Because the black church was growing and blacks were rapidly becoming more literate, they no longer had to rely totally on the metered hymn. Instead, they borrowed music from around them and revamped these songs to fit their own purposes and needs.

Choirs were established and hymnbooks began to appear. With the exception of two black poet-composers, Dr. Charles Albert Tindley and Lucie E. Campbell, the poets and composers were white. Of this group, certain composers became favorites among black congregations: Isaac Watts, Johnson Oatman, John Newton, Charles Wesley, Fanny Crosby and E. A. Hoffmann.

Among the all-time favorite hymns, which became known as "gospelized hymns or gospel hymns," are Crosby's "Jesus, Keep Me Near the Cross" and "Pass Me Not, O Gentle Savior," Watts' "At the Cross," Hoffman's "Leaning on the Everlasting Arms," Wesley's "Father, I Stretch My Hands to Thee," Newton's "Amazing Grace," and Oatman's "No, Not One" and "Higher Ground."

"Jesus, Keep Me Near the Cross" (#19), harmony by J. Jefferson Cleveland and Verolga Nix, contains many elements typical of black gospel music: "the flatted seventh," the "raised fourth," and the "raised second" (or "flatted third") scale steps; passing tones, compound chords, and chordal substitution. It has been set in 6/8 time, instead of 6/4, to make for easier reading. Despite the changes from the original setting, this composition is a hymn that a congregation can readily sing. A more gospelized version is sometimes heard that entails a change from 6/8 to 9/8 time, as well as a highly improved accompaniment against a basically unchanged melody. Improvise this hymn, both vocally and instrumentally.

"Jesus, Savior, Pilot Me" (#49) arranged by Verolga Nix is suitable for unison or solo performance, although a trained choir could perform it in parts. While set in triple meter, the chord values have been changed to resemble the manner in which this hymn is usually performed. Perform it slowly, with a lot of feeling, and bear in mind that the setting is contemporary gospel hymnody. Improvise at will.

Hymns Penned or Handed Down by Blacks

"Father, I Stretch My Hands to Thee" (#11) is representative of the many metered or lined hymns which were performed by blacks from about 1805-1900. These hymns were sung without accompaniment and were passed down from generation to generation. Therefore, no musical scores exist. Similarly, the chorded melody contained in *Songs of Zion* is provided as a mere guide.

The hymn definitely should be sung *a capella*. Disregard proper breathing, phrasing, and diction, for they destroy the concept of metered hymnody. As free harmony is a characteristic of this music genre, encourage it. It is important that one person intone two lines at a time, followed by singing from the entire congregation. There are other hymns that can be lined to the same meter and melody of "Father, I Stretch": "Amazing Grace," "I Heard the Voice of Jesus Say," "Am I a Soldier of the Cross," "I Love the Lord, He Heard My Cry," and "Alas! And Did My Savior Bleed."

"I Will Trust in the Lord," (#14) arranged by J. Jefferson Cleveland, has seldom, if ever been written down. While not a metered hymn, it also was passed down from generation to generation. Therefore, it is easy for congregations to learn, and unlimited improvisation is possible. This composition is sometimes referred to as a Negro spiritual and is effective as a solo. It is probably not a Negro spiritual, but simply one of those songs most black folk know.

All of the suggestions for "I Will Trust in the Lord" are applicable to "I Shall Not Be Moved" (#35). However, it is a congregational song, rather than a solo. It was often used in the Civil Rights Movement as a song of sure resolve. It is still needed for Christians to bolster their courage against the forces that pull us off course, and ask us to accept something other than the stance which we must take against racism, sexism, militarism, and the other "isms" that are contrary to our Lord's teachings.

The most prolific writer in black hymnody was Dr. Charles A. Tindley, whose productive period was 1900-1906. *Songs of Zion* contains twelve of Tindley's hymns, which are excellent for solo or congregational, and improvisatory use.

"Some Day," also known as "Beams of Heaven" (#10) should be sung slowly with great expression. Do not perform it in a cut and dried manner; *elongate the quick and short-value notes.* Improvise, both vocally and instrumentally.

"We'll Understand It Better By and By" (#55) is effective if sung fast, with a rocking beat. It is excellent for congregational use and should be highly improvised by vocalists as well as instrumentalists. The use of instruments, other than keyboard, is encouraged. This hymn can arouse the emotions of most congregations.

"Stand By Me" (#41) is one of Tindley's most popular hymns; however, this song is almost never performed as originally written. Because of this fact, it was arranged by J. Jefferson Cleveland and Verolga Nix to resemble the manner in which it is usually performed. Sing this hymn in parts, in unison or as a solo. It can be sung as a special selection during the service or used as altar call.

Negro Spirituals and Afro-American Liberation Songs

The earliest form of Afro-American religious music was the spiritual. We do not know exactly when spirituals began to appear on the scene. However, it is estimated that the development of this folk song began around 1775 and

129

continued until about 1875. This type of black religious music was created because the slaves had a message to share with one another and the entire world. Considering their bondage, vocal music was one of the safest and most effective means of slave expression. It is remarkable that more than 6,000 spirituals emerged from slavery. Just as remarkable is the fact that these songs were passed intact from generation to generation. These songs were created to be sung *a capella*, but they are appealing when sung with accompaniment.

"Roll Jordan, Roll" (#117) contains two of the identifying characteristics of the spiritual: the use of the flatted seventh and the naturalized seventh degrees of the scale in the same composition. This spiritual, which is written in the key of E-flat major, can easily be transposed to other keys, and should be performed at a moderate pace, but with vigor and strength. This spiritual is representative of the call-and-response chant, which involves a leader (soloist) and a group (choir or congregation) responding to a short, melodic statement by the leader.

"Lord, I Want to Be a Christian" (#76), arranged by Delores Lane, is an example of the slow, sustained, long phrase melody common to many spirituals. The melody has been slightly varied, the chordal progressions made interesting and rhythm varied to a small degree. Without alteration, it is appropriate for an organ or piano prelude, interlude, or offertory; a choir anthem, a congregational hymn, a solo, a small ensemble piece, or a service response. Perform it slowly and reverently, either with or without accompaniment. The dynamics may range from moderately soft to moderately loud or loud. Perform this spiritual as written, or if improvisation is used at all, keep it to a minimum. If performed vocally, stress good balance, harmony and blend. Remember that the theme of this hymn is Christian commitment.

"Hold On" (#86), arranged by J. Jefferson Cleveland,

represents the group of spirituals which have a syncopated, segmented melody and quick tempo. Intended for choral performance, sing this hymn as written, paying careful attention to the dynamic markings. "Hold On" can also be performed as a solo by omitting the choral sections. Some improvisation is recommended, especially at cadences throughout and at the end. Sing with conviction and fervor, for the themes of "Hold On" include perseverance, patience, belief, and courage. Do not change the wording; sing it in dialect, as written.

Some spirituals, such as "Woke Up Dis Mornin'" (#146) are similar in structure to the black gospel song, which indicates that the development of this medium was influenced by the spiritual. While this spiritual can be sung without accompaniment, its overall gospel flavor almost dictates an improvised keyboard accompaniment. In both songs, the chordal progressions are simple enough to allow easy improvisation. As "Woke Up Dis Mornin'" is a call-and-response chant, the leader should have a strong, vibrant voice. This is an easy song to teach to either the choir or congregation. The parts can be taught exactly as they appear in the score. Sing this lively song with enthusiasm.

A spiritual that allows for unlimited congregational improvisation is "Hush, Hush, Somebody's Callin' Mah Name" (#100). Perform this excellent congregational song unaccompanied with soft hand-clapping or foot-tapping to keep the rhythm going. Put no restrictions on its performance. Either unison or parts may be appropriate, depending upon the particular setting.

"He Nevuh Said a Mumbalin' Word" (#101) is a spiritual about Christ's Crucifixion. It is an easy melody with simple chord changes and is effective when sung as a solo, with guitar or autoharp accompaniment consisting of only the chord changes. A minor key was usually chosen by the slaves to depict sorrow, grief, pain, suffering, and humiliation. Unison singing by the congregation, with the same type of accompaniment, is also effective. If keyboard instruments are used, either *sustain or arpeggiate* the chord changes. Improvisation in this instance is really not needed and not recommended.

The thief who was crucified with Jesus was the impetus for the creation of "Do, Lord, Remember Me" (#119). Sing this excellent congregational song without accompaniment and with pronounced rhythmic movement. Part singing is recommended, although unison is effective. In order to achieve some variety, sing the first line of verses 2, 3 and 4 as a duet by a high and low voice, with everyone singing the remaining portions of each verse. Observe the accents to keep the rhythm flowing and pronounced.

Although "His Name So Sweet" (#90) and "Over My Head" (#167) have been arranged for male and female voices respectively, each can be successfully performed by the opposite voice, without having to make alterations. Perform these two spirituals as arranged with special emphasis on blend and the closeness of harmony. Emphasize the syncopation of "His Name So Sweet." If possible, let a vocalist with a natural tenor or high-pitched voice, sing the part of the leader. The tempo of this hymn should be rather fast, while that of "Over My Head" should be moderate. These two spirituals are most effective without accompaniment.

The creators of the spiritual seem to have favored using *altered scale degrees*. Whether they were conscious of these altered scales or not is immaterial. What is important is that secular music genres adopted these alterations as integral parts of their characteristic development; namely, the flatted third, sixth, and seventh. "My Lord! What a Mourning" (#145), contains the flatted sixth and seventh scale degrees. These alterations lend harmonic variety to the composition, without hindering the performance. It is recommended that the choir perform this spiritual in parts while the congregation sings the melody in unison.

J. Jefferson Cleveland's arrangement of "No Hidin' Place" (#141) written in the key of F major contains A-flat, D-flat and E-flat. Perform this spiritual as written, and use little instrumental improvisation.

Perhaps the most pronounced usage of the flatted seventh among the spirituals is found in the melody which accompanies the verses to "There's a Great Camp Meeting" (#156). Sing this "coded meaning" spiritual, which had both religious and political significance, without accompaniment and with much joy and spirit. The leader who may be female or male, must sing with vigor and emotion. The choral or congregational response should be as vigorous as the leader's solo parts.

"O, Mary, Don't You Weep, Don't You Mourn" (#153) is another "coded meaning" spiritual. Sing it at a rapid pace with jubilation and excitement. Though effective without accompaniment, a rousing piano or organ accompaniment, with a gospel swing, greatly enhances the excitement of this spiritual. It is excellent for congregational use, religious retreats, rallies, and sing-alongs. Improvise at will.

Little needs to be said about the text to "Oh, Freedom" (#102), for like "We Shall Overcome" (#127), it has been adopted by almost all nations. The word "freedom" has numerous connotations and is an important word to all nations and races. The Cleveland-Nix arrangement offers an optional melody which is appropriate when this spiritual is performed as a solo. This melody can also be performed as an obligato while the other four parts are being sung. Sung with or without accompaniment, it is a favorite of many congregations.

"Rockin' Jerusalem" (#103) is an exercise in syncopated rhythm. It is written in the key of A-minor (natural form) or the Aeolian mode. Sing this rousing song jubilantly and without accompaniment. Adhere strictly to the rhythm.

Two spirituals which are appropriate for religious celebrations are "Rise an' Shine" (#79) and "Jubilee" (#109). The word "jubilee" (often spelled and pronounced "juberlee") is an important one to the Afro-American, for it denotes social and spiritual freedom from slavery. Accordingly, most spirituals with a "jubilee" theme are lively. "Rise an' Shine" is no exception. Sing it with spirit and anticipation for the day when all of God's children will be free from bondage—the time of "juberlee." Sing this spiritual as written and, preferably, *a capella*.

The Cleveland arrangement of "Jubilee" allows the lower voices of the choir to respond to the higher voices. It is recommended that three women and three men from the congregation be taught the verses and sing them from the pews. This adds variety while giving the congregation a sense of participation in the song performed by a trained choir. Perform this spiritual *a capella* if the situation allows. If not, use instruments. Perform in such a way that a "march to freedom" is suggested.

Gospel Songs

The performance of black gospel music is an art, the core of which is improvisation. There are no restrictions on vocal or instrumental improvisation. However, one must use discretion in light of the composition being performed. Because this art is improvisational, printed manuscripts of gospel music usually are mere guides to the format of the composition and, for the most part, do not represent the actual sound of the composition. The performer has to make it sound the way it should.

The black gospel style couples the sacred and the secular, for the average gospel performer incorporates into this style direct elements of the spiritual, blues, jazz, pop, rock, and secular folk music. Flatted thirds, sixths, and sevenths; compound chords, arpeggios, trills, runs, turns, tremolos, glissandi, as well as inversions are found in modern gospel music. As far as improvisation is concerned there are no boundaries.

Gospel music has gone through periods of metamorphosis, resulting in various styles. In the early 1920s, Dr. Thomas A. Dorsey began the period of historic gospel. This period lasted until the late 1950s and included Roberta Martin, Lucie Campbell, Kenneth Morris, Theodore Frye, Doris Akers, and others. Among those bridging the gap between the historical gospel and modern gospel period which began in the late 1950s were Clara Ward, Dorothy Love Coates, James Cleveland, and Alex Bradford. The modern era of gospel includes, but not limited to, Edwin Hawkins, Jessye Dixon, Andrae Crouch, Dannibelle, R. Fryson, and Curtis Burrell. Both styles exist quite successfully side by side, neither hampering the popularity of the other.

One of the all-time favorites in the historic style is "Christ Is All" (#180) by Kenneth Morris. Elements of the spiritual are evident with the use of the flatted-third scale degree and the call-and-response concept. The manuscript remains fairly true to the way the song should be performed and can be performed as written. However, restricted improvisation is recommended. This gospel song is a favorite of black gospel choirs and black congregations. Piano or organ is almost a must; however, this does not preclude the use of other instruments. Although "Christ Is All" is often performed as a solo, it is more effective when sung by a choir or congregation.

Roberta Martin's arrangement of "Even Me" (#174) is a classic in the gospel genre. It is usually performed as a solo. This song can stir any congregation to unlimited emotional heights. Because of the high tessitura of the refrain, a voice of high range creates more excitement than a low-ranged voice. A simple but beautiful song that lends itself to much improvisation, it is often performed as a prayer response or altar call selection.

Another classic from the historic era of black gospel is "He Understands, ["He'll Say 'Well Done' "] (#178) by Lucie E. Campbell. Performed at many funerals, it is simply written, easy to sing, and well known by Christians of all denominations. Its popularity is due, in large part, to its text, which speaks to the inevitable end of life and the understanding Christ who will receive those who have believed and struggled on this side of terra firma. This gospel hymn has been subjected to numerous arrangements—some slow and serene, some fast and exciting. Whatever the nature of the arrangement, this song is effective whether performed by a soloist, a choir, an ensemble, or a congregation. "Ad libitum" ("at will") is a most appropriate term for this song. Improvisation is certainly in order.

Undoubtedly, Thomas A. Dorsey's "Precious Lord, Take My Hand" (#179) is the most popular black gospel song ever written. Dr. Martin Luther King, Jr. adopted this as one of the "movement for freedom and racial equality songs." Hence, its popularity was expanded the world over. The simple, appealing melody makes this song a favorite among soloists, the medium through which it is most often performed. One of the most emotion-rendering songs in Christianity, perform "Precious Lord . . ." with considerable feeling. To get the maximum *soul* from this song, experiment with instrumental and vocal improvisation.

Clara Ward's "How I Got Over" (#188) is representative of the transition period between the historic and modern eras of black gospel. Therefore, it contains elements of both styles. It is a fast gospel song containing many more chromatics than the gospel songs of the historic period. Its design is a direct parallel to a fiery preacher delivering a rousing sermon to the most receptive and emotional congregation, which responds with enthusiastic shouts of thanksgiving. In performing this gospel song, pull out all of the stops.

As it is not easy to pen a song of this nature exactly as it is to be performed, a word of caution is in order: the music is different from any recording of this song. Even the recordings by the composer differ from the written manuscript. This is a trait that is typical of the majority of black gospel songs, due to their highly improvisatory nature. In order to produce creative instrumental improvisation, it is imperative to study this song carefully before performing it.

Margaret Douroux possesses the ability to write modern gospel songs which are within the musical grasp of most congregations, and "What Shall I Render?" (#190) is a case in point. It is almost hymn-like in style, has an appealing, easy to learn melody, and closely-knit harmonies. It can be performed as written or improvised, and can easily be sung by choir and/or congregation. Begin in the key of F major and modulate to G major, A-flat major, and B-flat major. Sing the entire song in F major and only verse 1 in the rest of the keys. Sing in parts and with accompaniment. This is a most appropriate song to sing while tithes and offerings are being received.

"God Has Smiled on Me" (#196) by Isaiah Jones is a well-known gospel song among black choirs and congregations. Following its introduction, begin the piece by singing the refrain with "ooh," without a repeat; then sing the refrain with words and with the repeat. Add an obligato by having a select ensemble of women's voices duplicate the tenor part an octave higher than written. Congregations pick up the refrain to this gospel song very quickly, even in parts, so have them sing along with the choir and soloist. Improvise at will, especially the keyboard accompaniment.

"Lord, Help Me to Hold Out" (#194) by James Cleveland was an instant success when recorded. The text, which prays for God's continual guidance, is one of the major reasons this gospel has been so popular. Sing this hymn in parts, using little vocal improvisation. Improvisation of the keyboard enhances the beauty of the piece and is recommended. The tempo marking reads "slow and stately," however, do not pace the tempo too slowly.

Walter Hawkins' "Goin' Up Yonder" (#181) is another gospel song that became well-known almost instantaneously. The version of "Goin' Up Yonder," contained in the hymnbook, is basically a four-part harmonization with the chords written on the treble staff. Transposition is highly recommended because of the ranges. Sing in parts. A more elaborate arrangement for solo with choral background is available and is written in the key of D-flat major. Improvise, especially on keyboard, without restriction. Stress the syncopation and perform it at a moderate tempo.

Andrae Crouch is one of the most prolific writers of modern gospel and wrote "Soon and Very Soon" (#198). The song's very nature is such that any one could learn it just from hearing it. Its beauty is its musical simplicity. The chordal progressions are very conventional, the melody is charming and it makes for a gospel masterpiece. Congregations and choirs have no problem singing this song. The tempo can be march-like, signifying the march of Christians into the promised land, or a little faster, signifying the jubilation of going home.

"Move Me" (#185) by Richard Alan Henderson is one of the most recent and beautiful gospels contained in *Songs of Zion*. It is elaborately arranged and should be performed by a trained choir or ensemble with an excellent soloist. The modulation from the hymn-like choral part to the solo is smooth and unproblematic. This is an excellent example of the workable fusion of the black gospel style and the

European classical style. Vocally, we recommend no improvisation of the first selection, optional improvisation of the solo, and no improvisation of the special refrain. The keyboard role can be improvised if desired. However, the piece can be performed well as written. Remain aware of the syncopation which occurs throughout.

Songs for Special Occasions

This section of *Songs of Zion* was compiled with the more accomplished musician in mind; that is, the trained soloist, the accomplished choir or vocal ensemble, the trained director, the accomplished pianist and/or organist. The musical compositions contained herein are arranged accordingly. While minimal consideration was given to congregational participation, a few of these compositions lend themselves to such participation. Sub-classifications represented in this section are: (1) Anthems, (2) Negro Spirituals Arranged in Anthem Style, (3) Specially-Arranged Hymns in Choral Style, and (4) Solo Arrangements.

Anthems

Lena McLin is one of the most prolific composers and arrangers of our time. Her quasi-contemporary setting of "Praise God From Whom All Blessings Flow" (#204) is suitable for several occasions because of its brevity. If performed as an anthem, sing it twice, *a capella*. It can also be sung as a choral interlude, a choral offertory, or as a benediction. Perform it as written, observing carefully all of the dynamic markings.

Negro Spirituals Arranged in Anthem Style

Volume II of the *Dett Collection of Negro Spirituals*, compiled and arranged by the late eminent composer,

R. Nathaniel Dett, includes "We Are Climbing Jacob's Ladder" (#205) set in anthem form. Dett arranged this spiritual for a trained vocal ensemble. The treble voices are set in duo style, while the bass notes are set in longer, rhythmic values than the three upper voice parts. The tenor part echoes the soprano and alto parts, thereby forming a type of broken canon line. Dett has cleverly used the African call-and-response technique in a four-part vocal European classical setting. As is indicated in the score, perform this composition *a capella* and with the vocal group possessing good voices.

The arrangement of "Go Down, Moses" (#212) by J. Jefferson Cleveland also retains the call-and-response technique. The soloist, preferably a baritone or tenor, intones the "call" and the choir gives the "response" in four parts. This arrangement is intended for a soloist with mixed choir and not for congregational use. Interpret all dynamic markings as indicated and perform the composition as written. Only two verses are scored; however, if the director desires more verses, he/she may choose from sixteen additional ones found in the traditional version (#112). This will create more variety and lengthen the song. Perform this anthem *a capella*.

Specially-Arranged Hymns in Choral Style

"Blessed Quietness" (#206) by W. S. Marshall, as arranged by J. Jefferson Cleveland and Verolga Nix, remains in hymn-style; yet it is quite different from the original. While the original setting is in triple (3/4) meter, this hymn is almost always sung in quadruple (4/4) meter, as it is set here. Though embellished throughout, the four musical lines remain intact and singable, making this hymn suitable for congregational participation. Sing it with spirit and joy, improvising both vocally and instrumentally in a black gospel style.

J. Jefferson Cleveland has arranged William B. Bradbury's "Just As I Am" (#208) in a quasi-modern style that includes chordal suspensions and compound chords. Following the chordal introduction, which can also be used as an interlude between verses, the main body of the song retains, for the most part, the original melody. This makes the hymn suitable for congregational singing as well as for special vocal ensembles or for the choir. Only two verses of the original hymn are included in this setting; however, if more are desired, they can be taken from the original version in the former Methodist *Book of Hymns*, or any standard hymnal.

Solo Arrangements

Will L. Thompson's "Jesus Is All the World to Me" (#216) takes on a new guise as arranged by Verolga Nix. The melody remains traditional, with the exception of three measures and the final cadence. The accompaniment transforms this familiar hymn into a beautiful solo arrangement. Set in a smooth, arpeggiated style, the melody is pronounced; and yet, there is a great deal of variety in the accompaniment. An accomplished soloist, together with an accomplished pianist or organist, could make this the highlight of any worship service. Improvisation is not necessary, for the activity found in the accompaniment is enough. The simply-arranged melody against the busy accompaniment makes for excellent internal contrast. This versatile solo can be used in many different segments of the service.

J. Jefferson Cleveland's solo arrangement of John Newton's "Amazing Grace" (#211) combines an embellished melody in the black style with an independent accompaniment written in the modern European classical style. The embellished melody and independent accompaniment are beautifully constructed, each enhancing the other. The soloist must interpret the vocal line "ad libitum" (at will or freely). The accompaniment is suitable for piano or organ. Perform the accompaniment with feeling. Though there are many arrangements of this familiar hymn, this setting possesses a freshness that is unique.

Service Music

Introits

"One God, One Faith, One Baptism" (#220) by Garel C. Smith and J. Jefferson Cleveland is a short choral introit which a congregation can learn without difficulty. Its beauty comes from its simplicity and closely-knit harmonies. It is most effective *a capella*. This is an excellent introit (or response) for baptism, confirmation, or general worship services. Perform as written.

Offertories

Odel Hobbs, eminent choral music specialist, composed "We Give Thee What We Have, Lord" (#229) especially for *Songs of Zion*. Its melody is simple and appealing; its harmonies basically conventional, with a bit of modern harmony interspersed; and its text meaningful and easy to learn. Congregations will enjoy performing this offertory with the choir. Perform as written, either with or without accompaniment.

Responses

"Remember Me" (#235), harmonized by J. Jefferson Cleveland is an excellent congregational prayer response. Composed during the slave era "Remember Me" is easy for congregations to learn because of its simplicity.

Lengthen the response by adding verses from "Amazing Grace," "I Heard the Voice of Jesus Say," "Father I Stretch My Hands to Thee," "Must Jesus Bear the Cross Alone?" and "At the Cross." Although accompaniment may be used, it is more moving when performed *a capella* and in parts.

Benedictions

"Doxology" (#238) by J. Edward Hoy is arranged with three-fourths of the composition sung in unison. Although a change from quadruple meter to triple meter occurs, the change does not disrupt the 'flow of the music. A bit of canonic treatment is seen in the *alleluia* section while the amen section is written in block chordal harmony. A delightful, festive benediction, sing it *a capella*.

Amens

Verolga Nix's "Amen" (#241) is set in a lively, calypso style. Although intended for performance by a trained choir, a congregation can learn the melody in a relatively short time. During its performance, pronounce the syncopation, the characteristic feature of this composition. The chordal progressions are conventional and the vocal ranges are comfortable. For effectiveness, perform "Amen" with a calypso-styled accompaniment.

X

Afterword: When Sunday Comes: "Walk Together Children"

Sunday does come—every week. It offers us anew a chance to celebrate the Lord's rising and our rising. It presents us with an opportunity to gather as the children of God around the Word and the sacrament. It is the Lord's Day—the day of his resurrection, and our day "to serve the Lord with gladness." And we can come into that Presence with singing and praise and thanksgiving; we can sing the Songs of Zion, even in a strange land.

When Sunday comes next, it does not have to be a designated festival day for there to be celebration. Every Sunday is a special day; a time to rehearse the gracious acts of God. Every Sunday is a season of the gospel and every season is a time to remember and re-experience God's acts of grace on which salvation is grounded and hopes renewed for years to come. In the words of the ancient prayer in the black tradition, Sunday is "once more and again that your humble servant comes knee-bowed and body bent before the throne of grace to thank you for last night's lying down and this morning's rising . . . for touching me with a finger of love and waking me up in due time . . . for keeping me from dangers, seen and unseen . . . and letting me live yet in a gospel land . . . and the blood is still running warm in our veins."

Sunday is an opportunity to remind those who know and

145

those who have forgotten and to inform those who never knew what God has done and continues to do through the Holy Spirit: offering gifts of grace—and grace upon grace. Worship provides the occasion to accept what God has done for us. Then we really are free to worship, to praise God, to act. Sunday gives us the chance to be reminded of gifts that we cannot create but only accept. We can recognize the futility of our efforts and yet rejoice in God's victories. We can "lift every voice and sing, till earth and heaven ring!" [SOZ #32 and #210]

That is what this book has been about and why it is presented to the readers: to encourage diversity in our prayer, praise, and preaching; to enrich the liturgical life of the church; to reflect the rainbow in our worship; and to walk together as children of God on earth—rehearsing here at the Lord's Table for the eschatological Feast to be set at the Welcome Table. It is an invitation to all to understand and appreciate the Songs of Zion and to sing them, but also to value the liturgical tradition and context out of which they come. The liturgy is not what we do; it is who we are. These acts of worship can broaden our liturgical genres. The songs are the voices of the soul that can help strangers and pilgrims to celebrate on the journey. They can help us focus on the present with its continuing demands and perplexities, provide strength and moral stamina for facing these realities and grant us an ever-present hope for a future that will be dominated by the presence of love, peace and justice for all of God's children.

Come Sunday was written for those who plan and conduct worship—clergy and lay, white, black, Native American, Asian, Hispanic, European, African—all who would lend some refulgence to the gathering of God's people when Sunday comes. It does not have to be liturgical "ho-hum" nor last Sunday's ritualistic tedium where nothing happened because nobody expected anything to happen or planned for anything to happen or wanted anything to happen. Sunday does come, and each time offers a chance to be creative and to try new songs and new ways of singing and praying and preaching. I am not suggesting simply trying to imitate or duplicate, but rather to learn from a tradition and to appropriate it in your own way. This book is designed to improve worship. Let me illustrate from a recent service I attended.

There was something different about the communion service. Everybody said so. I heard the comments from various people: "This was a lively service." "There was spirit here today." "I enjoyed communion for the first time." Said one elderly white pastor to me as we left the college gymnasium where we had worshiped: "I'm sure glad we finally got some life in the communion service. What happened?" The difference was the singing and the songs chosen and the way we sang them. The Pastor preached as well as he always preaches. The communion ritual was the same used in previous years. What happened was that the worship committee had sat down and looked at the service with an eye toward inclusiveness. They took a page from *Come Sunday* and learned that Communion Sunday in the black church is not a Sunday to be dreaded or avoided; rather, it is the Sunday of the month to look forward to. It is the Sunday that the once-a-month attenders don't want to miss. It is a Sunday with the highest attendance. In the black tradition, communion is not viewed as a *funeral service for a dead Jesus* requiring quietness and solemnity. It is not even viewed as a memorial meal. Rather, it is a time of joyful celebration of the victorious risen Christ over sin and death and all of the powers of hell! We've come through Friday with all of its pain, suffering scourging and death, then Sunday comes. God sends Sunday to celebrate the victory of the forces of God & Company over the sinister powers of Pilate and the Good Friday crowd. God claimed the victory for us all, Hallelujah! It is time to sing joyfully, to praise God with

shouts of triumph. It is time to sing with Charles Albert
Tindley:

> I am free from, condemnation,
> Jesus' blood has made me free,
> I am now a new creation,
> Hallelujah, He saves me.
>
> I believe it, I believe it,
> Jesus died to set me free.
> On the cross He bought my pardon,
> Hallelujah, He saves me!
>
> [SOZ #43]

It is time at Communion to sing "Christ Is All" [SOZ
#180] and to know that "It Is Well With My Soul":

> My sin—oh, the bliss of this glorious thought:
> My sin, not in part but the whole,
> Is nailed to the cross and I bear it no more,
> Praise the Lord, praise the Lord, O my soul.
>
> It is well with my soul,
> It is well with my soul.
>
> [SOZ #20]

And indeed, we did sing these and other songs that
helped us testify to the reality of the risen Christ in the
breaking of bread and drinking wine on our knees. We went
forth from that place praising God together [SOZ #88]. Our
hunger and thirst were satisfied and our lives restored
("Hungry and Thirsty, Lord, We Come" [SOZ #245]. We
left energized, enabled, empowered, and compelled to
witness that HE is a heart-fixer and a mind-regulator who
requires all who call upon his name and accept his grace to
show forth his love and work for justice in the land.

On further reflection, maybe the preaching was different.

I seem to remember there being more passion and freedom in the preacher's delivery. He didn't leap off the pinnacle of the temple, though; nor did he only speak *to* the congregation gathered. There were no gimmicks or bags of tricks or imitative magic. He simply preached *in* and *for* the congregation gathered around the Word and Sacrament. He preached with urgency and zeal as one whose heart was on fire, and we all were able to say "Yes" to the Word from the Lord. We were one in the spirit and one in the Lord as the Liturgy of Zion became an imperceptibly integrated and integral part of this inclusive worship experience. And the people said: "A-men!" Some merely said it in their hearts, but the African-Americans who left that service had another way of saying what happened. They said: "We *had* church!"

A Liturgy

The suggestions provided here are intended for use on the Sunday following January 15. The readings are from the Common Lectionary, *the Second Sunday After Epiphany, with an alternative gospel reading provided.*

If it is impractical to print the service for use by the congregation, the leader may read the responses alone.

GREETINGS

Leader: We have genuflected before the god of science.

People: **only to find that it has given us the atomic bomb.**

Leader: We have worshiped the god of pleasure,

People: **only to discover that thrills play out and sensations are short-lived.**

Leader: We have bowed before the god of money,

People: **only to learn that there are such things as love and friendship that money cannot buy.**

All: **Only God is able.**

Leader: Is someone here moving toward the twilight of life and fearful of that which we call death?

People: **Why be afraid? God is able.**

Leader: Is someone here on the brink of despair because of the death of a loved one, the breaking of a marriage, or the waywardness of a child?

151

People: **Why despair? God is able to give us the power to endure that which cannot be changed.**

Leader: Is someone here anxious because of bad health?

People: **Why be anxious? Come what may, God is able.**

All: Surely God is able.[1]

HYMN—"Glory Be to Our God on High" (*Songs of Zion*, 2)

or

"God of Grace and God of Glory"

COLLECT

Leader: Let us pray.
Gracious God,
you have made of one blood all nations of the earth
and by the blood of the cross have redeemed all that
you have created.
Fill us with the wisdom and the strength to establish
justice and righteousness in every aspect of life.
that your people may dwell in peace and security
all their days; through Jesus Christ our Lord.

People: **Amen.**

OLD TESTAMENT LECTION—Isaiah 62:1-5

PSALM—Psalm 36:5-10

or

Psalter No. 577, "May Righteousness Flourish"

EPISTLE LECTION—I Corinthians 12:1-11

ANTHEM or HYMN

If a hymn is used, "In Christ There Is No East or West" (Supplements to The Book of Hymns, *911*) *is appropriate.* (*Alternative tunes: "McKee"* [Songs of Zion, *65*]; *"St. Peter"* [Book of Hymns, *192*])

---

1. Adapted from Martin Luther King, Jr., "Our God Is Able," in *Strength of Love* (New York: Pocket Books, 1968). Copyright © 1963 by Martin Luther King, Jr. Copyright © 1968 by Coretta Scott King. Used by permission of Joan Daves.

A Liturgy

GOSPEL LECTION—John 2:1-11
or
Luke 19:37-44

SERMON

HYMN—"Lift Every Voice and Sing" (*Songs of Zion*, 32)
"Where Cross the Crowded Ways of Life"

INTERCESSIONS
Free intercessions or the following form of guided prayer may be used.

Leader: We remember the conviction of Martin Luther King, Jr., that "freedom is never voluntarily given by the oppressor; it must be demanded by the oppressed." Therefore let us pray for courage and determination on the part of those who are oppressed, particularly our sisters and brothers in South Africa. . . .

We remember Martin's warning that "a negative peace which is the absence of tension" is less than "a positive peace which is the presence of justice." Therefore let us pray that those who work for peace in our world may cry out first for justice. . . .

We remember Martin's insight that "injustice anywhere is a threat to justice everywhere. We are caught in an inescapable network of mutuality tied in a single garment of destiny. Whatever affects one directly affects all indirectly." Therefore let us pray that we may see nothing in isolation, but may know ourselves bound to one another and to all people under heaven. . . .

We remember Martin's lament that "the contemporary church is often a weak, ineffectual voice with an uncertain sound. It is so often the arch-supporter of the status quo. Fra from being disturbed by the presence of the Church, the power structure of the average community is consoled by the Church's silent and often vocal sanction of things as they

153

are." Therefore let us pray that neither this
congregation nor any congregation of Christ's
people may be silent in the face of wrong, but that we
may be disturbers of the status quo when that is
God's call to us. . . .

We remember Martin's "hope that dark clouds of
racial prejudice will soon pass way and the deep fog
of misunderstanding will be lifted from our
fear-drenched communities and in some not too
distant tomorrow the radiant stars of love and
brotherhood will shine over our great nation with all
their scintillating beauty." Therefore in faith, let us
commend ourselves and our work for justice to the
goodness of Almighty God. . . .[2]

THE PEACE

OFFERING

PRAYER OF THANKSGIVING

If the Lord's Supper is celebrated the first three petitions of the
PRAYER OF THANKSGIVING may be adapted and incor-
porated into Great Thanksgiving 20 in At the Lord's Table,
following the words "It is fitting to give you thanks and
praise."

Leader: O God, our help and our hope:
For all who from the beginning of time have cared
for the poor, the neglected, the oppressed, and the
outcast,

People: **We praise your name.**

Leader: Particularly for your servant, Martin, for his selfless
devotion to the establishment of racial justice, and
for his determination to pursue world peace, to the
very sacrifice of his life,

People: **We praise your name.**

Leader: For all who continue in the struggle despite hardship,
misunderstanding, and ridicule.

---

[2] Quotations are from Martin Luther King, Jr., *Letter from Birmingham*
City Jail (Philadelphia: American Friends Service Committee, 1963),
pp. 3, 5, 8, 13, 15.

People: **We praise your name.**

Leader: Above all, for Jesus Christ who came to preach good news to the poor, to proclaim release to the captives, to set at liberty the oppressed.

People: **We praise your name.**

Leader: Through Christ, with Christ, and in Christ, we offer the prayer of the whole Church:

THE LORD'S PRAYER

HYMN—"We Shall Overcome" (*Songs of Zion*, 127)

or

"There Is a Balm in Gilead"

DISMISSAL WITH BLESSING

Leader: We are not alone in this vast, uncertain universe. Beneath and above the shifting sands of time, the uncertainties that darken our days, and the vicissitudes that cloud our nights is a wise and loving God.[3] In the name of this gracious God, go forth with good courage. And the blessing of God, holy and undivided Trinity, be with you now and always.

People: **Amen.**

---

[3] From Martin Luther King, Jr., "Antidotes for Fear," in *Strength to Love* (New York: Pocket Books, 1968). Copyright © 1963 by Martin Luther King, Jr. Copyright © 1968 by Coretta Scott King. Used by permission of Joan Daves.

This service was prepared by Dr. William B. McClain and Dr. Laurence Hull Stookey, professors of preaching and worship at Wesley Theological Seminary, Washington, D.C.

Discography

The following works will be helpful in providing a more specific example of "creative interpretation" by both pioneers in gospel as well as contemporary artists. Many of the earlier recordings are not available at this time.

Christ Is All Trad. "Gospel Soul of Sam Cook—Volume 2" Specialty Records 2128

Even Me Trad. "Mahalia Jackson" Kenwood Records 8493

Contemp. "Down Memory Lane" (Rev. James Cleveland) Savoy 14311

Give Me a Clean Heart "Go" (Shirley Caesar) Myrrh Records B-6665

God Be With You Trad. "Precious Lord: The Beloved Songs of Thomas Dorsey" Columbia GK 32151

Contemp. "Deleon" (Deleon Richards) Myrrh (LP) 6804

God Has Smiled on Me "Rev. James Cleveland Presents the Voices of Tabernacle" Savoy 14352

God's Amazing Grace Trad. "Tiny Crumbs of Happiness" (Dr. T. Brown) Morada Records 108

Contemp. "Amazing Grace" (Aretha Franklin) Atlanta Records SD2-906

Goin' Up Yonder "Love Alive" (Walter Hawkins) Light
   Records El-60095

He Knows Just How Much We Can Bear Trad. "Clara
   Ward Memorial Album" (Clara Ward) Savoy 14308
   Contemp. "New Dawning" (Maceo Woods) Stax 14007

He'll Understand and Say Well Done Trad. "The Best of
   the Davis Sisters" Savoy 7017
   Contemp. "He Promised New Life" (Donald Vails)
   Savoy 14753

How I Got Over Trad. "Mahalia Jackson" Kenwood
   Records 8598
   Contemp. "Amazing Grace" (Aretha Franklin) Atlanta
   Records SD2-2906

I Don't Care What the World May Do "He Lifted Me"
   (Alex Bradford) Specialty Records 2143

I Don't Feel No Ways Tired "Rev. James Cleveland &
   Salem Inspirational Choir" Savoy 7015

I'll Fly Away "Oh, Lord Stand By Me" (The Five Blind
   Boys) Specialty Records 2123

Just to Behold His Face Trad. "The Best of Dorothy Love
   Coates" Specialty Records 2141
   Contemp. "B. L. and S. Singers" Savoy 14740

Lord Don't Move This Mountain "Inez Andrews" MCA
   Records 2649

Lord Help Me to Hold Out "Rev. James Cleveland Presents
   Harold Smith and the Majestics" Savoy 14319

Lord Touch Me "The Best of the Wards Singers" Savoy
   7015

Old Ship of Zion Trad. "The Old Ship of Zion" (Roberta
   Martin) Kenwood Records 507
   Contemp. "It's Gonna Rain" (Milton Brunson) Myrrh
   Records 6696

Only a Look Trad. "The Best of Roberta Martin Singers"
   Savoy SGL 7018
   Contemp. "What's He Done for Me" (Rev. Clay Evans)
   Savoy 14762

Precious Lord Trad. "Precious Lord: The Beloved Gospel Songs of Thomas A. Dorsey" Columbia Records KG 32151

    Contemp. "Rev. James Cleveland and the Metro Mass Choir" Savoy 7067

Soon and Very Soon "Live in London" (Andrae Crouch) Light 60073

Surely God Is Able "The Best of the Ward Singers of Philadelphia, Pa." Savoy 7015

The Blood Will Never Lose Its Power "Take the Message Everywhere" Light 5504

Trees "Pentecostal Community Choir" Savoy 7053

Until I Found the Lord Trad. "The Famous Ward Singers" SVG Records 5001

    Contemp. "Love Alive 2" (Walter Hawkins) Light E1-60074

What Shall I Render "James Cleveland Presents Triboro Mass" Savoy 14525

Yes, God Is Real Trad. "Yes, God Is Real" (Rev. Cleophus Robinson) Savoy 14648

    Contemp. "More Than Wonderful" (Sandi Patti) Heart Warming Records 3818

Selected Bibliography

Barbour, Floyd, Editor. *The Black Seventies*. Boston: Beacon Press, 1970.

Botkin, B. A., editor. *Lay My Burden Down:* A Folk History of Slavery. Chicago: University of Chicago, 1945.

Caldwell, Gilbert H. *Race, Religion and Reconciliation*. Philadelphia: Martin Press, 1989.

Cone, James H. *The Spirituals and the Blues*. New York: Seabury Press, 1972.

Cone, James H. *God of the Oppressed*. New York: Seabury Press, 1975.

Dett, R. Nathaniel. *Religious Folk Songs of the Negro*. Hampton, Va.: Hampton Institute Press, 1927.

Dixon, Christa K. *Negro Spirituals: from Bible to Folksong*. Philadelphia: Fortress Press, 1976.

DuBois, W. E. B. *The Souls of Black Folk*. New York: Fawcett World Library, 1961, 1903.

Dubois, W. E. B. *The Gift of Black Folk*. New York: Johnson Reprint Corporation, 1968, 1924.

Fisher, Miles Mark. *Negro Slave Songs in the United States*. New York: Russell, 1968, 1953.

Frazier, E. Franklin. *The Negro Church in America*. New York: Shocken Books, 1964.

Gadsden, James S., Editor. *Experiences, Struggles, and Hopes of the Black Church*. Nashville: Tidings Press, 1975.

Harding, Vincent. *There Is a River:* The Black Struggle for Freedom in America. New York: Harcourt Brace Jovanovich, 1981.

Heilbut, Tony. *The Gospel Sound*. New York: Simon and Schuster, 1971.

Hickman, Hoyt, Saliers, Donald, Stookey, Laurence H. *The Handbook of Christian Worship*. Nashville: Abingdon Press, 1986.

Johnson, James Weldon. *God's Trombones*. New York: Penguin Books Reprint, 1969, 1927.

Johnson, James Weldon and Johnson, J. Rosamond. *The Books of American Negro Spirituals*

Jones, Major. *Black Awareness: A Theology of Hope.* Nashville: Abingdon Press, 1971.

Jones, Ralph H. *Charles Albert Tindley: Prince of Preachers.* Nashville: Abingdon Press, 1982.

Lake, Kirsopp, translator. *The Apostolic Fathers.* Cambridge: Harvard University Press, 1965.

Lincoln, C. Eric. *Race, Religion and the Continuing American Dilemma.* New York: Hill and Wang, 1984.

Lincoln, C. Eric. Editor. *The Black Experience in Religion.* New York: Anchor Books, 1977.

Lincoln, C. Eric. *The Black Church Since Frazier.* New York: Anchor Books, 1983.

Mays, Benjamin and Nicholson, J. W. *The Negro's Church.* New York: Institute of Social and Religious Research, 1933.

Mays, Benjamin Elijah. *The Negro's God.* New York: Atheneum, 1969.

Mbiti, John S. *African Religions and Philosophies.* New York: Anchor Books, 1970.

McClain, William B. "What Is Authentic Black Worship?" in *Christianity and Crisis.* October, 1972.

McClain, William B. *Black People in the Methodist Church: Whither Thou Goest?* Cambridge: Schenkman Publishing Company, 1984.

McClain, William B. *Travelling Light: Christian Perspectives on Pilgrimage and Pluralism.* New York: Friendship Press, 1981.

McClain, William B. *The Soul of Black Worship.* Madison, New Jersey: Multi-Ethnic Center Press, 1981.

McClain, William B. "Good News, the Kingdom's Coming" in *Military Chaplain's Review.* Volume 12. Number 1. March, 1983.

McClain, William B. "Black People in United Methodism: Remnant or Residue?" in *Quarterly Review.* Nashville: The Methodist Publishing House. Spring, 1984.

Mitchell, Henry H. *Black Preaching.* New York: J. B. Lippincott, 1970.

Mitchell, Henry H. *Black Belief.* New York: Harper & Row, 1975.

Raboteau, Albert J. *Slave Religion.* New York: Oxford University Press, 1980.

Richardson, Cyril, editor. *Early Christian Fathers.* Philadelphia: Westminster Press, 1953.

Rogers, Jefferson P. "Black Worship: Black Church" in *The Black Church.* Boston: Black Ecumenical Commission Press, 1972.

SEASONS OF THE GOSPEL. Nashville: Abingdon Press, 1979.

Shaughnessy, James P., Editor. *The Roots of Ritual.* Grand Rapids: Wm. B. Erdman Press, 1976.

Songs of Zion. See especially the narrative introductions to the sections on hymns and spirituals: J. Jefferson Cleveland, "A Historical Account of the Hymn in the Black Worship Experience" [pp. 1-4]; J. Jefferson

Cleveland and William B. McClain, "A Historical Account of the Negro Spiritual" [pp. 73ff.]; and J. Jefferson Cleveland, "A Historical Account of the Black Gospel Song" [pp. 172ff.].

Southern, Eileen. *The Music of Black Americans*. New York: W. W. Norton, 1971.

Spencer, Jon Michael, Editor. *The Journal of Black Sacred Music*. Durham: Duke University Press. Volumes I-V, 1988-90.

Thurman, Howard. *Jesus and the Disinherited*. Nashville: Abingdon Press, 1949.

Thurman, Howard. *Deep River* and *The Negro Spiritual Speaks*. Richmond, Ind.: Friends United Press, 1975.

Traynham, Warner. *Christians Faith in Black and White:* A Primer in Black Theology. Boston: Parameter Press, 1973.

Wilmore, Gayraud. *Black Religion and Black Radicalism*. New York: Doubleday, 1972.

Work, John Wesley. *Folk Songs of the American Negro*. New York: Bonanza Books, 1940.

Footnotes

I

[1] Hortense J. Spillers, "Martin Luther King and the Style of the Black Sermon," *The Black Scholar*, Vol. 3, No. 1, September 1971.

II

[1] B. A. Botkin, ed., *Lay My Burden Down: A Folk History of Slavery* (Chicago: University of Chicago Press, 1945), p. 27.

[2] Ibid., p. 82.

[3] Ibid., p. 151.

[4] "O Day of Rest and Gladness," Christopher Wordsworth, 1807-1885.

[5] Laurence H. Stookey, "Keeping Time: The Church and the Lectionary," (Washington, D.C.: Wesley Theological Seminary, 1987), p. 2.

[6] Cyril Richardson, ed., *Early Christian Fathers* (Philadelphia: The Westminster Press, 1953), p. 287.

[7] Kirsopp Lake, trans., *The Apostolic Fathers* (Cambridge: Harvard University Press, 1965), p. 397.

[8] Hoyt L. Hickman, Donald Saliers, Laurence G. Stookey, eds., *The Handbook of Christian Worship*, (Nashville: Abingdon Press, 1986): See also *Seasons of the Gospel: Resources of the Christian Year* (Nashville: Abingdon Press, 1979, pp. 73ff.; See also the numerous writings of James F. White, Professor of Liturgy, University of Notre Dame.

III

[1] William B. McClain, *Black People in the Methodist Church: Whither Thou Goest?* (Abingdon Press, 1990), pp. 19-20.

[2] Robert Anderson, *From Slavery to Affluence: The Memories of Robert Anderson, Ex-Slave*, (Hemingford, Neb., 1927), p. 22-23.

[3] Gayraud Wilmore, *Black Religion and Black Radicalism* (New York: Anchor Books, year), pp. 113-14.

[4] Benjamine E. Mays and J. W. Nicholson, *The Negro's Church* (New York: Institute of Social and Religious Research, 1933), p. 37.

IV

[1] William B. McClain, "What Is Authentic Black Worship?" *Christianity and Crisis,* October, 1970. See James S. Finney, "Doctrinal Differences Between Black and White Pentecostalists," *Spirit* (Vol. 1, No. 1) July, 1977.

[2] Marner R. Traynham, *Christian Faith in Black and White* (Boston: Parameter Press, 1973), p. 92.

[3] Union United Methodist Church, Boston, (then Fourth Methodist) separated from the Bromfield Methodist Church in 1819 in order that blacks could practice a more emotional religion. They were urged by their fellow white Methodists to establish their own church.

[4] James A. Joseph, "Has Black Religion Lost Its Soul?" *The Black Seventies,* ed. Floyd Barbour (Boston: Beacon Press, 1970), p. 70.

[5] Jefferson P. Rogers. "Black Worship: Black Church," *The Black Church,* Vol. 1 (Boston: Black Ecumenical Press, 1972), pp. 64-65.

[6] James P. Shaughnessy, ed., *The Roots of Ritual* (Grand Rapids: Wm. B. Eerdman Press, 1973), p. 86.

[7] Program for Christmas Concept, Fifth Avenue Presbyterian Church, New York City, Dec. 25, 1965.

[8] Charles Albert Tindley was the Methodist pastor of what is now known as Tindley Temple United Methodist Church, Philadelphia, from 1902 until his death in 1933. Dr. Tindley is credited with writing the first gospel songs to be published, "Stand By Me," and "We'll Understand It Better By and By" both in 1905 (pp. 41 and 55 in *Songs of Zion*).

[9] Leroi Jones (Imamu Baraka) *Blues People* (New York: Grove Press, 1975), p. 27.

V

[1] Cf. John S. Mbiti, African Religions and Philosophies (New York: Anchor Books, 1970), pp. 37-49.

[2] Hortense J. Spillers, "Martin Luther King and the Style of the Black Sermon," *The Black Scholar,* Vol. 3, September 1971, pp. 14-27.

[3] J. H. Jackson, "Annual Address," National Baptist Convention, U.S.A., (Chicago: 1962).

[4] James Weldon Johnson, "Listen Lord," *God's Trombones* (New York: Penguin Books The Viking Press), 1976, pp. 13-14.

VIII

[1] Robert E. Parks, *Race and Culture* (New York: Free Press, 1964), p. 63.

[2] John Wesley Work, Folk Songs of the American Negro (New York: Bonanza Books, 1940), p. 88.

Scripture Index to Songs of Zion

Topical Index to
Songs of Zion

Climbin' Up d' Mountain, 120
Fix Me, Jesus, 122
On Ma Journey, 157
I Don't Feel No Ways Tired, 175
He Understands, He'll Say "Well Done", 178
Surely God is Able, 193

Praise of God
Little David, Play Your Harp, 94
Mah God is So High, 105

Prospect of Death
Study War No More, 138
I Feel like My Time Ain't Long, 148
I Stood on de Riber ob Jerdon, 149
Precious Lord, Take My Hand, 179

Providence of God
I Know Who Holds Tomorrow, 29
His Eye is on the Sparrow, 33
God Be With You, 37
My Heavenly Father Watches Over Me, 69
He's Got the Whole World in His Hands, 85
Didn't My Lord Deliver Daniel?, 106
God is So Good, 140
Even Me, 174
God has Smiled on Me, 196
Blessed Quietness, 206
Thank You Lord, 228

Repentance and Return
Lord, I'm Coming Home, 18
Standin' in the Need of Prayer, 110
Only a Look 197
Just As I Am, 208

Return of the Lord
It is Well with My Soul, 20
Battle Hymn of the Republic, 24
Over My Head, 167
Soon and Very Soon, 198

The River
Jesus, Keep Me Near the Cross, 19

On Jordan's Stormy Banks, 54
Deep River, 115
Roll, Jordan, Roll, 117
Ev'ry Time I Feel the Spirit, 121
Precious Lord, Take My Hand, 179

The Saints
What are They Doing in Heaven, 63
Joshua Fit de Battle of Jericho, 96
Peter, Go Ring Them Bells, 97
Mary and Martha, 162

Salvation from Sin
Glory to His Name, 4
Father, I Stretch My Hands to Thee, 11
I Believe It, 43
My Secret of Joy, 51
Throw Out the Lifeline, 56
I Have Found at Last the Savior, 60
Love Lifted Me, 71
He Touched Me, 72
Calvary, 87
Glory, Glory Hallelujah, 98
Come out de Wilderness, 136
King Jesus is a-Listenin', 152
Certainly, Lord, 161
I Know the Lord's Laid His Hands on Me, 166
Even Me, 174
Until I Found the Lord, 177
Give Me a Clean Heart, 182
The Blood Will Never Lose Its Power, 184
How I Got Over, 188
Old Ship of Zion, 189
Footprints of Jesus, 200
Yes, God is Real, 201
My Faith Looks Up to Thee, 215
Jesus is All the World to Me, 216

The Spirit
I'm Gonna Sing, 81
Ev'ry Time I Feel the Spirit, 121

The Storms of Life
Stand By Me, 41

He Understands, He'll Say "Well Done", 178

Unity of All People

Jesus Loves the Little Children, 26

In Christ There is No East or West, 65

A Prayer for Love, 70

He's Got the Whole World in His Hands, 85

De Gospel Train, 116

Worship and Adoration

Let All Mortal Flesh Keep Silence, 217

O Worship the Lord, 219

Communion Music for the Protestant Church, 243

Gloria in Excelsis, 244

Zion, City of God

We're Marching to Zion, 3

Rockin' Jerusalem, 103

Great Day, 142

I Want to Be Ready, 151

Oh! What a Beautiful City, 169

How I Got Over, 188

264.076

M1262

LINCOLN CHRISTIAN COLLEGE AND SEMINARY

111386

Printed in the United States
27790LVS00002B/31

9 780687 088843

3 4711 00195 9636